DEDALO AGENCY

SPAIN
Travel guide

HOW TO PLAN
A TRIP TO SPAIN
WITH BEST TIPS
FOR FIRST-TIMERS

Edited by: Domenico Russo and Francesco Umbria
Design e layout: Giorgia Ragona
Book series: Journey Joy

Spain Travel guide
How to Plan a Trip to Spain
with Best Tips for First-Timers

www.agenziadedalo.it

SPAIN
Travel guide

Foreword

In the following pages of the book, you will find essential advice on what to see and do in Spain, and there will be specific insights to enjoy your trip to the fullest (even without spending exorbitant amounts).

The travel guide series of the Journey Joy collection was designed to be lean and straight to the point. The idea of keeping the guides short required significant work in synthesis, in order to guide the reader towards the essential destinations and activities within each country or city.

If you like the book, leaving a positive review can help us spread our work. We realize that leaving a review can be a tedious activity, so we want to give you a gift. Send an email to **bonus@dedaloagency.net**, attach the screenshot of your review, and you will get completely **FREE**, in your mailbox, **THE UNRELEASED EBOOK**: "The Art of Traveling: Essential Tips for Unforgettable Journeys".

Remember to check the Spam folder, as the email might end up there!

We thank you in advance and wish you to always travel and enjoy every adventure!

Index

· · · · · · · · · ·

FOREWORD   4
INTRODUCTION   11
CHAPTER 1: MADRID   17

⋮ The Prado Museum   18
⋮ Retiro Park   19
⋮ Madrid's Royal Palace   20
⋮ Gran Vía   20
⋮ San Miguel Market   21
⋮ Santiago Bernabeu Stadium   22
⋮ Almudena Cathedral   22
⋮ Madrid Nightlife   23
⋮ Thyssen-Bornemisza Museum   24
⋮ Day Trip to Toledo   24
⋮ Madrid Cuisine   25
⋮ Final Thoughts   26

CHAPTER 2: BARCELONA   31

⋮ Sagrada Familia   32
⋮ Park Güell   33
⋮ Gothic Quarter   34
⋮ Barcelona's Beaches   35
⋮ La Rambla   35
⋮ Picasso Museum   36
⋮ Casa Batlló   37
⋮ Barcelona Nightlife   38
⋮ Day Trip to Montserrat   38
⋮ Camp Nou   39
⋮ Barcelona Cuisine   40
⋮ Final Thoughts   41

CHAPTER 3: SEVILLE   45

The Alcázar   46
Seville Cathedral and Giralda   47
Plaza de España   48
Triana District   48
Metropol Parasol   49
María Luisa Park   50
Seville Bullring   50
Day Trip to Jerez   51
Flamenco Show   52
Torre del Oro   52
Seville Cuisine   53
Final Thoughts   54

CHAPTER 4: VALENCIA   59

City of Arts and Sciences   60
Valencia Cathedral   61
Central Market   62
Turia Gardens   63
La Lonja de la Seda   63
Bioparc Valencia   64
The Albufera Natural Park   65
Day Trip to Altea   65
Fallas Museum   66
Valencia's Silk Exchange   66
Valencia Cuisine   67
Final Thoughts   68

CHAPTER 5: BILBAO   73

Guggenheim Museum   74
Casco Viejo   75
Bilbao Fine Arts Museum   76
Artxanda Funicular   76
San Mamés Stadium   77
Day Trip to Gaztelugatxe   77
Plaza Nueva   78
Bilbao Riverside Walk   79
Azkuna Zentroa   79
Bilbao's Bridges   80

Bilbao Cuisine — 81
Final Thoughts — 82

CHAPTER 6: GRANADA — 87

The Alhambra — 88
Albayzín — 89
Sacromonte — 90
Granada Cathedral — 91
Royal Chapel of Granada — 91
Day Trip to Sierra Nevada — 92
Generalife — 93
Granada's Street Art — 93
Hammam Al Ándalus — 94
Carrera del Darro — 94
Granada Cuisine — 95
Final Thoughts — 96

CHAPTER 7: SANTIAGO DE COMPOSTELA — 101

Santiago Cathedral — 103
The Legendary Camino de Santiago — 104
City of Culture of Galicia — 105
Mercado de Abastos — 106
Alameda Park — 106
Day Trip to Cape Finisterre — 107
The Old Quarter — 108
The University — 108
The Way of St. James — 109
Hostal dos Reis Católicos — 109
Santiago Cuisine — 110
Final Thoughts — 111

CHAPTER 8: SAN SEBASTIÁN — 117

La Concha Beach — 118
Old Town — 119
Monte Igueldo — 120
San Sebastián International Film Festival — 120
San Telmo Museum — 121
Day Trip to Pasaia — 122
La Bretxa Market — 122
Peine del Viento — 123

INDEX — 7

Miramar Palace   124
Tabakalera   124
San Sebastián Cuisine   125
Final Thoughts   126

CHAPTER 9: CÓRDOBA   131

The Mezquita   132
Alcázar de los Reyes Cristianos   133
Medina Azahara   134
The Roman Bridge   134
The Courtyards   135
Day Trip to the Sierra de Hornachuelos   136
The Jewish Quarter   136
Córdoba Synagogue   137
Calahorra Tower   137
The Flower Street   138
Córdoba Cuisine   139
Final Thoughts   140

CHAPTER 10: SPANISH CUISINE   145

The Tapas Culture   146
Seafood   147
Olive Oil   147
Traditional Dishes   148
Spanish Wines   149
Spanish Cheeses   150
Spanish Desserts   150
Spain's Food Markets   151
Vegetarian and Vegan Options   152
Sustainable Food Practices   152
Final Thoughts   153

CHAPTER 11: HOW TO TRAVEL SPAIN ON A BUDGET   159

Budget Accommodation   160
Eating on a Budget   160
Public Transport   161
Free Attractions   162
Budget Shopping   162
Cheap Flight and Train Tips   163
Discount Cards   163

Off-Season Travel   164
Final Thoughts   164

CHAPTER 12: 10 CULTURAL EXPERIENCES
YOU MUST TRY IN SPAIN   **169**

1 - Flamenco Show   170
2 - Spanish Fiestas   170
3 - Bullfighting   171
4 - Spanish Art   171
5 - Wine Tasting   172
6 - Traditional Crafts   172
7 - Spanish Language   173
8 - Spanish Sports   173
9 - Spanish Music   174
10 - Spanish Architecture   174

CONCLUSION   **177**
FINAL NOTES   **181**

Introduction

Welcome, dear traveler, to your quintessential guide to the enchanting splendors of Spain! An enthralling journey awaits you in this country where past and present collide in a vibrant spectacle of cultures, landscapes, flavors, and rhythms. With this guide, we invite you to embark on an odyssey that delves into the heart and soul of Spain, unearthing the multi-faceted charms that make this country a destination of timeless allure.

Our journey starts by immersing ourselves in the pulsating heart of Spain, the capital city, Madrid, explored in Chapter 1. Witness the royal grandeur of Palacio Real, discover masterpieces at the Prado Museum, and feel the energy of Plaza Mayor. Traverse through the vibrant markets, explore the city's rich history whispered by its streets, and treat your taste buds to the gastronomic delights that are uniquely Spanish.

Chapter 2 transports you to the sun-kissed beaches and architectural wonders of Barcelona. Gaze in awe at the surreal creations of Gaudí, get lost in the Gothic Quarter's narrow lanes, and enjoy the city's buzzing nightlife. Barcelona, with its vibrant culture and dynamic cityscape, is a canvas painting a vivid tale of history, art, and Catalan spirit.

The magnetic allure of Seville is explored in Chapter 3. Feel the passion of flamenco, be enchanted by the Moorish charm of the Alcazar, and experience the fervor of Feria de Abril. Seville's rhythm and allure are sure to cast a spell on you.

In Chapter 4, we navigate through the beauty of Valencia, a city where the futuristic City of Arts and Sciences resides in harmony with the medieval charm of the Old Town. Be captivated by Valencia's blend of old and new, and don't miss the chance to indulge in an authentic Paella Valenciana in its birthplace.

Chapter 5 leads us to the artistic and culinary hub of Bilbao. Home to the iconic Guggenheim Museum and boasting a thriving food scene, this city is the soul of the Basque Country. Bilbao's unique blend of traditional and avant-garde will leave you yearning for more.

In Chapter 6, we journey south to Granada, where the Alhambra's majestic silhouette against the Sierra Nevada will captivate your senses. Granada is a historic gem where every corner tells a story of its Moorish past.

Chapter 7 unveils the spiritual Santiago de Compostela, the culmination of the famous Camino de Santiago pilgrimage. Its stunning cathedral, ancient streets, and spiritual aura make Santiago a city of unique spiritual and cultural significance.

Chapter 8 transports you to the seaside city of San Sebastián, a gastronomic paradise tucked away in Spain's northern Basque Country. From its breathtaking La Concha beach to its renowned pintxos, San Sebastián is a treat for your senses.

Córdoba, in Chapter 9, is a tapestry of history and culture. Explore the mesmerizing Mezquita, wander through the Judería, and experience the vibrancy of the Fiesta de los Patios. Córdoba is a living testament to Spain's diverse cultural history.

Chapter 10 is a culinary journey through the flavors of Spain. From the smoky essence of a well-made paella to the succulent taste of jamón ibérico, and from the sweet delight of churros to the refreshment of sangria, Spanish cuisine is a narrative of its regions, its history, and its people.

Chapter 11 provides essential tips and advice on exploring Spain with a savvy eye on your budget. This practical guide arms you with valuable insights on transportation options, affordable accommodations, cost-effective eateries, and free attractions.

Finally, Chapter 12 immerses you in unique Spanish cultural experiences. Learn how to flamenco dance, participate in a Spanish cooking class, join a local fiesta, or walk a portion of the Camino de Santiago. These experiences will not only create unforgettable memories but also provide an intimate under-standing of the passionate Spanish spirit.

This guide is your passport to an unforgettable journey through Spain's kaleidoscope of experiences. As you delve into its diverse landscapes, rich history, vibrant culture, and delicious cuisine, you'll find Spain unveiling its many facets, letting you in on its secrets and traditions. By the end of your journey, you'll carry a piece of Spain within you, a cherished memory that will beckon you to return to this extraordinary land. Let's go – your Spanish adventure awaits!

CHAPTER 1:
Madrid
· · · · · · · · · · · · ·

Welcome to the magnetic heart of Spain, Madrid! Spain's largest city and capital, Madrid, exudes an irresistible energy that seizes every visitor from the moment they set foot on its streets. A city that never sleeps, Madrid is a vibrant symphony of culture, history, art, gastronomy, and nightlife. A place where every winding alley has a story to tell, and every grand square is a stage set for life's countless dramas to unfold.

As the sun shines brightly on the city, Madrid reveals itself in all its grandeur. Ornate Baroque buildings stand tall alongside sleek modern structures, creating a cityscape that effortlessly blends tradition and modernity. Streets lined with chestnut trees echo with the sound of life, from the clink of coffee cups in sun-drenched terraces to the banter of Madrileños as they go about their day.

The city's cultural richness is unparalleled. Madrid is home to some of the world's greatest museums, such as the Prado, Reina Sofia, and Thyssen-Bornemisza, boasting incredible collections of European art. In the heart of Madrid, art isn't confined to museums; it spills out onto the streets, coloring everything from grand buildings to hidden alleyways with a creative touch. Madrid is also a city of green spaces. The city's parks, like the expansive Retiro Park, are perfect refuges from the urban hustle. These parks are not just places of relaxation, but also bustling hubs of activities, where you can row a boat, see a free concert, or explore a rose garden.

No matter how many times you've been here, Madrid always has something new and unexpected to offer. It might be a hidden tapas bar, a charming boutique, a secret garden, or an impromptu flamenco performance on the streets. That's the beauty of Madrid - it's a city that encourages you to explore and rewards you with delightful surprises at every turn.

And when the sun sets, Madrid truly comes alive. It's a city famous for its late nights, where tapas bars buzz with conversation, theaters hum with anticipation, and nightclubs pulse with the latest beats. From quiet wine bars to lively flamenco shows, Madrid's nightlife is as diverse as it is thrilling.

Whether you're an art enthusiast, a food lover, a history buff, or a partygoer, Madrid offers an experience tailored just for you. As we journey through this captivating city, you'll discover that Madrid is not just Spain's capital; it's a living, breathing entity that celebrates life in all its forms. So, hold on tight as we dive into the energetic heart of Spain, exploring the places, tastes, and experiences that make Madrid an unforgettable destination.

The Prado Museum

Welcome to the crown jewel of Madrid's art scene, the Prado Museum. Stepping into the hallowed halls of the Prado is like embarking on a journey through the annals of European art history. Housed in an imposing Neo-Classical building, the Prado's collection spans over 8,000 paintings, including works from Spanish masters like Velázquez, Goya, and El Greco, along with other renowned artists such as Rubens and Titian.

The Prado isn't just a gallery; it's a timeless testament to human creativity, where every canvas whispers a tale from the past. As you wander through its corridors, you'll come face to face with art pieces that have shaped Western art's narrative. Not to be missed are Velázquez's "Las Meninas", Goya's "The Third of May 1808", and Bosch's "The Garden of Earthly Delights".

Given the museum's vast collection, it's wise to plan your visit ahead of time. Decide which masterpieces you'd like to see, or opt for a guided tour for a more immersive experience. Remember that the museum is free in the evenings from Tuesday to Saturday and all day on Sundays.

Retiro Park

In the heart of Madrid, the Retiro Park serves as the city's green lung, a tranquil oasis amidst the urban hustle. Covering 125 hectares and home to over 15,000 trees, this vast park offers a welcome respite to locals and tourists alike. It's a place where joggers weave their paths through tree-lined trails, families picnic under leafy canopies, and lovers row boats across the tranquil Retiro Pond.

Beyond its natural beauty, the park also boasts architectural gems like the Crystal Palace, a stunning glass and iron structure that hosts contemporary art exhibitions. The Rose Garden, bursting into colors during spring, and the Monument to Alfonso XII, overlooking the grand pond, are other key attractions worth exploring.

Retiro Park is a year-round destination, each season offering a unique charm. However, the park truly comes alive during weekends when locals descend en masse, filling the air with laughter, music, and cheer. Don't forget to check out the book fair held every spring and the free concerts in the summer.

Madrid's Royal Palace

Standing tall on a bluff overlooking the river Manzanares, the Royal Palace of Madrid is an epitome of opulence and a testament to Spain's regal past. It's the largest royal palace in Western Europe by floor area, a stunning representation of Baroque and Classicism architecture.

The palace's sumptuously decorated rooms, with their luxurious furnishings, fine tapestries, and exquisite porcelain, reflect the splendor of the Spanish monarchy. The highlights of the palace include the Throne Room, the Royal Armoury, and the Hall of Mirrors. A visit to the palace isn't complete without stepping into its beautiful gardens, the Campo del Moro and Sabatini Gardens.

Although the palace isn't the official residence of the king, it's used for state ceremonies, so ensure it's open to the public on your visit day. The palace offers free entry during certain hours for EU citizens, and it's advisable to get there early to avoid long queues. Audio guides are available to enrich your exploration of this grand edifice.

Gran Vía

Madrid's Gran Vía is more than a street; it's a bustling microcosm of the city's vibrant spirit. Often referred to as Madrid's Broadway, Gran Vía is the city's entertainment epicenter, its buildings housing theatres, cinemas, and retail stores. Architecturally, Gran Vía is a parade of eclectic styles, with stunning examples of Art Deco, Neo-Mudejar, and Modernist buildings lining its stretch.

Strolling down Gran Vía is like walking through a living tapestry of Madrid's history. Every corner, every building has a story to tell. Highlights include the Telefónica Building, a towering skyscraper from the 1920s, and the Edificio Metrópolis, a stunning French-inspired building crowned with a glistening dome. Whether you're shopping, catching a show, or simply soaking up the atmosphere, Gran Vía pulsates with energy round the clock. Remember that most stores close in the afternoon for siesta and reopen in the evening. And while the street is safe, it's always wise to be mindful of your belongings in crowded areas.

San Miguel Market

In the heart of Madrid's old town, the San Miguel Market stands as a testament to the city's culinary prowess. This early 20th-century iron market is a gastronomic paradise, with over 30 stalls offering a plethora of Spanish delicacies. From fresh produce and seafood to tapas, pastries, and a selection of wines, the market is a feast for the senses.

As you wander through the market, take time to sample some of the best flavors Spain has to offer. Taste the melt-in-your-mouth jamón ibérico, savor the freshness of a seafood paella, or indulge in a glass of chilled cava.

The market is bustling at all hours, but it's particularly vibrant in the evening when locals gather for drinks and tapas. It's advisable to visit with an empty stomach and an open mind, ready to dive into the Spanish culinary scene. Note that the market can get crowded, so patience is key.

Santiago Bernabeu Stadium

No visit to Madrid is complete without a pilgrimage to the Santiago Bernabeu Stadium, the hallowed home ground of Real Madrid. Whether you're a football enthusiast or not, touring this iconic stadium is a mesmerizing experience. With a seating capacity of over 80,000, the stadium is one of the world's most prestigious football grounds.

The Bernabeu tour takes you on a journey through the history of Real Madrid, one of the most successful clubs in football. You'll get to visit the players' tunnel, the bench, the dressing rooms, and even step onto the pitch. The tour also includes a visit to the Trophy Room, a testament to the club's illustrious history.

Tours run daily, and it's advisable to book tickets in advance, especially during the football season. If you're lucky, you might even catch a live game, a spectacle that's sure to give you goosebumps. Remember that the stadium is enormous, so wear comfortable shoes for the tour.

Almudena Cathedral

Facing the Royal Palace, Almudena Cathedral is a symbol of Madrid's spiritual heart and a testament to the city's architectural prowess. Although its construction began in 1879, the cathedral was only completed in 1993, making it one of the newest grand churches in Europe. The fusion of various architectural styles, including Gothic revival on the exterior and Neo-Romanesque in its crypt, reflects the time span across which it was built.

Within the cathedral, your gaze will undoubtedly be drawn upwards, where the vaulted ceilings display a unique blend of traditional and contemporary designs. The stained glass windows and beautifully painted cupola add to the cathedral's serene atmosphere, inviting quiet reflection amidst the city's hustle and bustle.

Don't miss the chance to visit the cathedral's museum where you can delve into Madrid's religious history and ascend to the dome for a panoramic view of Madrid's cityscape. Remember to dress respectfully as this is still an active place of worship.

Madrid Nightlife

When the sun sets, Madrid truly comes to life. Madrid's nightlife, famous throughout Spain, offers a variety of experiences from the pulsating energy of nightclubs to the traditional tapas bars tucked away in the city's narrow streets. Madrid is known for its late-night dining culture, where locals often start their dinner well past 9 PM, followed by a night of revelry.

A trip to Madrid would be incomplete without experiencing a live flamenco show. These passionate performances of dance, music, and song are an integral part of Spanish culture. Venues like Corral de la Morería and Casa Patas offer unforgettable flamenco shows that capture the spirit and fervor of this traditional art form.

Remember that Madrid's nightlife starts late and goes on until the early hours of the morning. Pace yourself, hydrate, and remember that the Madrid metro operates until 1:30 AM, and night buses run all night for your convenience.

Thyssen-Bornemisza Museum

Completing Madrid's Golden Triangle of Art, the Thyssen-Bornemisza Museum is a must-visit for art enthusiasts. The museum's collection is one of the most extensive and diverse in Madrid, comprising more than 1,000 artworks from the 13th to the late 20th century. Here, you can explore everything from medieval art to contemporary pieces, including significant works from the Renaissance, Baroque, and Impressionist periods.

The museum houses works by great masters such as Rubens, Rembrandt, Degas, Renoir, Van Gogh, and Picasso. Notably, it hosts an exceptional collection of American paintings, which is unique in European museums. For modern art lovers, movements such as Pop Art, Expressionism, and European avant-garde are well-represented.

Audioguides are available in various languages and are a great way to deepen your understanding of the artworks. The museum also offers free entry on Monday afternoons, but expect larger crowds during this time. The museum's shop is a great place to pick up art-themed souvenirs.

Day Trip to Toledo

Just a stone's throw away from Madrid, Toledo, the City of Three Cultures, awaits. A UNESCO World Heritage site, Toledo is a splendid blend of Christian, Jewish, and Muslim influences that have left their mark over centuries. Its historic center, perched on a hill above the Tagus River, is a labyrinth of narrow streets, home to an array of monuments spanning various architectural styles.

Take time to visit the imposing Alcázar, a stone fortification at the city's highest point. Walk through the narrow alleys of the Jewish Quarter, with its synagogues and the Sephardic Museum. Visit the cathedral, a masterpiece of Gothic architecture, and take in the serenity of the Mosque of Cristo de la Luz, a symbol of Toledo's multicultural heritage.

Day trips to Toledo can be easily arranged from Madrid, either by bus, train, or organized tours. Make sure to wear comfortable shoes as Toledo's streets can be steep and cobbled. And don't leave without trying the city's famous marzipan!

Madrid Cuisine

Madrid is a gastronomic paradise, where traditional Spanish dishes meld with international influences, resulting in a flavorful fusion that will delight any foodie. Begin your culinary exploration with a visit to one of the city's bustling food markets, such as Mercado de San Miguel or Mercado de San Antón. Here you can sample a smorgasbord of Spanish treats, from tapas and pintxos to fresh seafood and delectable pastries.

Tasting Madrid's signature dishes is a journey in itself. Savor the cocido madrileño, a hearty stew of meats and vegetables that is perfect for Madrid's cooler months. Bite into a bocadillo de calamares, a calamari sandwich that is a staple of Madrid's street food. And, of course, you can't leave without trying the churros con chocolate, a favorite Spanish dessert.

Madrid is also a great place to try Spain's world-famous wines. Whether you prefer the robust reds of Rioja, the crisp whites of Rueda, or the bubbly delights of Cava, Madrid's bars and restaurants offer a wine for every palate.

When dining in Madrid, remember that locals usually have late dinners, often starting around 9 or 10 PM. Tipping is not mandatory in Spain, but leaving a few coins is a good practice in restaurants. Lastly, don't forget to explore Madrid's burgeoning vegan and vegetarian scene, with a growing number of restaurants catering to plant-based diets.

Final Thoughts

Your journey through Madrid only marks the beginning of the richness that Spain has to offer. This metropolis of joy, with its vibrant life, profound history, and diverse culture, is a microcosm of the country. As you wander through its streets, don't forget to stray off the beaten path. Explore neighborhoods like Malasaña, known for its alternative scene, or La Latina, where you can experience Madrid's best Sunday flea market, El Rastro.

While the city's main attractions are a must-visit, Madrid's charm is also found in the everyday life, in the sidewalk cafes, in the warmth of its people, in the rhythm of its nightlife. It's a city that never sleeps yet always dreams, a city that embraces the future without forgetting its past.

Remember to make the most of Madrid's excellent public transportation system. The metro, buses, and suburban trains make it easy to move around the city and its surrounding areas. Also, consider getting the Madrid Tourist Travel Pass for unlimited travel on public transport.

As you leave Madrid, remember that Spain's diversity extends beyond its capital. The fiery passion of Andalusia, the rugged landscapes of Extremadura, the modernist beauty of Catalonia - every region holds its own unique allure. So, as you say adiós to

Madrid, say hola to the rest of Spain. Let your Spanish journey continue to surprise you, to teach you, to inspire you. Madrid is not the end; it's just the beginning. Vamos, let's keep exploring!

CHAPTER 2:
Barcelona
· · · · · · · · · · · · · · · · · · ·

Nestled between the Mediterranean Sea and the hills of Montjuïc, Barcelona sparkles with a vibrancy and style all its own. Catalonia's proud capital, a city of sun-dappled beaches, awe-inspiring architecture, and vibrant streets, Barcelona beckons with its unique charm and boundless energy. As Spain's second-largest city, it is a metropolis where centuries-old history and innovative design intertwine, creating a tapestry of experiences that captivate every kind of traveler.

Barcelona is perhaps most famous for its association with the celebrated architect Antoni Gaudí, whose masterpieces like the Sagrada Familia and Park Güell, dot the city's landscape. Gaudí's imagination and creativity have left a profound mark on Barcelona, and his distinctive modernist style adds a whimsical touch to the city's skyline. The curved lines, bright colors, and intricate details of his works have become synonymous with Barcelona's identity.

But Gaudí's creations are just the tip of the iceberg. The city's historic Gothic Quarter, or Barri Gòtic, takes you back in time, its labyrinthine alleys telling stories of Roman settlements, medieval splendor, and cultural transformations. Visit the magnificent Barcelona Cathedral, explore the remnants of the ancient Roman city at the History Museum, or simply lose yourself in the quarter's atmospheric cobblestone streets.

Barcelona's past is always within your reach, whispering tales of bygone eras.

Yet, Barcelona is not a city stuck in time. It's a hub of innovation and creativity, reflected in its dynamic food scene, its penchant for avant-garde design, and its thriving arts and music culture. The city's museums pay homage to the likes of Picasso and Miró, while its music festivals attract world-renowned artists. Barcelona's many markets and restaurants offer culinary delights, from traditional Catalan cuisine to global gastronomy, making it a food lover's paradise.

Barcelona is a city of contrasts, where tradition and innovation exist side by side. Its diverse neighborhoods, each with their own personality, offer endless opportunities for exploration. From the trendy beachfront district of Barceloneta to the bohemian Gràcia, the upscale Eixample to the vibrant Raval, Barcelona is a city of a thousand faces.

Above all, Barcelona is a city that knows how to live. Whether it's strolling along the sun-kissed beaches, relaxing in a terrace café on Las Ramblas, tasting tapas in a bustling market, dancing the night away in a club, or simply sitting in a quiet square watching the world go by, there's always a way to enjoy life in Barcelona. So let's start this journey, dive into the soul of Catalonia, and discover what makes Barcelona such an enchanting city.

Sagrada Familia

Imposing, intricate, and incomparable, the Sagrada Familia stands as a testament to Antoni Gaudí's visionary genius. Begun in 1882, this architectural marvel remains unfinished to this day, yet it's one of the most iconic landmarks of Barcelona. This colossal basilica, a fusion of Gothic and curvilinear Art Nouveau forms, presents a breathtaking panorama of towers, facades, and interior spaces richly adorned with religious symbolism.

Inside, the Sagrada Familia is a symphony of light and color. The forest-like columns reach up to the star-studded ceiling, while the spectacular stained-glass windows imbue the basilica with a magical glow. The Nativity Facade tells the story of Jesus' birth, life, and teachings, the Passion Facade portrays his suffering and death, and the Glory Facade, still under construction, will represent the path to God.

Buying tickets online in advance is highly recommended to avoid long queues. An audioguide is available, which gives insightful details into Gaudí's vision and the basilica's complex symbolism. Remember to dress respectfully, as the Sagrada Familia is a consecrated place of worship. Climbing one of the towers offers panoramic views of Barcelona, but requires a separate ticket.

Park Güell

Another of Gaudí's masterpieces, Park Güell, is a public park system composed of gardens and architectonic elements perched on Carmel Hill. Originally intended as an exclusive housing estate, the project was unsuccessful, but the resulting park is a UNESCO World Heritage Site that draws millions of visitors each year. This enchanting park is a fusion of natural landscapes and architectural innovations, all infused with Gaudí's unique style.

As you wander through the park, you'll encounter whimsical structures like the dragon-styled mosaic salamander "El Drac", the undulating ceramic tile bench, and the gingerbread-like gatehouses. The elevated square offers panoramic views over Barcelona, and the columned hall beneath, designed to be a market, is an architectural marvel.

The Monumental Zone, which houses most of Gaudí's creations, requires a ticket. However, the surrounding gardens and areas are freely accessible. Tickets for the Monumental Zone often sell out during peak tourist season, so it's advisable to book online in advance. The park is quite hilly, so wear comfortable shoes and bring water, especially in summer.

Gothic Quarter

Stepping into Barcelona's Gothic Quarter is like stepping into a time machine, where narrow, winding streets lead you through centuries of history. This is the oldest part of the city, where remnants of Roman walls stand beside medieval monuments. It's a place where every corner, square, and alleyway has a story to tell, making it a must-visit for history enthusiasts.

The heart of the Gothic Quarter is the magnificent Barcelona Cathedral, a stunning example of Gothic architecture. Nearby, the remnants of the Roman Temple of Augustus and the ancient Jewish Quarter, or "El Call", speak of Barcelona's diverse historical layers. Plaça del Rei, a medieval public square, is said to be where Columbus was received after his voyage to America.

Walking tours are an excellent way to explore the Gothic Quarter, as local guides can provide insight into the area's rich history. It's worth noting that while the area is generally safe, it's known for pickpockets, so keep an eye on your belongings. Numerous small shops, cafes, and restaurants line the streets, offering ample opportunities for rest and refreshment.

Barcelona's Beaches

Barcelona's location on Spain's northeastern coast ensures a vibrant beach scene, a delightful balance between urban life and seaside relaxation. The city's coastline stretches over 4.5 kilometers and is divided into several distinct beaches, each offering its unique atmosphere and attractions. Whether you're a sun worshiper, an avid swimmer, or simply enjoy beachside cafes, Barcelona's beaches are a paradise.

The most popular is Barceloneta Beach, known for its golden sand, lively atmosphere, and excellent seafood restaurants. Further north, Nova Icaria Beach is more peaceful and family-friendly, while Mar Bella Beach is known for its water sports facilities and a separate nudist area. Bogatell Beach, popular among locals, offers a quiet respite from the crowded city.

Visiting early in the morning or late afternoon can help avoid the peak crowds, especially during summer. Beach facilities are well-maintained, including showers, restrooms, and beach bars, or 'chiringuitos.' Be aware of your belongings, as beaches can attract opportunistic thieves. Also, remember that while Barcelona's beaches are beautiful, they are also urban beaches – for pristine, natural beaches, consider a day trip along the Costa Brava.

La Rambla

La Rambla, a bustling tree-lined boulevard stretching from Plaça de Catalunya to the waterfront, is the pulsating heart of Barcelona. This vibrant pedestrian street, divided into several sections, is a hive of activity day and night, brimming with shops, cafes, flower stalls, street artists, and performers. It's a place where locals and tourists converge, making it an essential part of the Barcelona experience.

Key attractions along La Rambla include the grand Liceu Theatre, one of Europe's leading opera houses, and the colorful Mercat de la Boqueria, a food market where you can sample a wide range of Spanish delicacies. Towards the southern end, the Maritime Museum and the Columbus Monument mark the historic gateway to the Mediterranean.

While La Rambla is a must-visit, it can be crowded and is known for overpriced restaurants and tourist traps. Keep an eye on your belongings, as pickpockets may operate in the area. Consider exploring the side streets and alleys branching off La Rambla, which lead into the Gothic Quarter and the trendy Raval neighborhood.

Picasso Museum

Dedicated to the life and works of Pablo Picasso, the Picasso Museum in Barcelona is an essential destination for art enthusiasts. Located in the hip El Born district, the museum is housed in five adjoining medieval palaces, an aesthetic match to the artistic treasures within. With over 4,000 works, it boasts one of the most extensive collections of Picasso's artworks, tracing his artistic journey from the early years to his final works.

Highlights include the Blue Period paintings, the iconic Las Meninas series, and numerous sketches and ceramics that reveal Picasso's creative process. While Picasso's later, more famous works are not well represented, the museum offers a deep understanding of his formative years and his strong connection with Barcelona.

It's recommended to book tickets online in advance to avoid queues. The museum offers free entry on Thursday afternoons and the first Sunday of every month, but these times can be busy. An audio guide is available, offering in-depth commentary on Picasso's artworks and life. Also, don't miss the temporary exhibitions, which often feature works by Picasso's contemporaries.

Casa Batlló

In Barcelona's elegant Eixample district, Casa Batlló is a shining example of Antoni Gaudí's distinctive architectural style. This UNESCO World Heritage site, often dubbed the 'House of Bones' for its skeletal facade, is an explosion of colors, shapes, and imagination. Its design, filled with symbolism and inspired by nature, is a testament to Gaudí's genius.

The building's interior is as impressive as its facade. From the whimsical staircases to the aquatic-themed rooms, each detail is meticulously crafted. The roof terrace, shaped like the back of a dragon, offers panoramic views of the city. The building's transformation from a conventional house into an artistic masterpiece speaks volumes about Gaudí's vision.

When planning a visit, consider buying tickets online in advance to avoid queues. The 'Gold Priority' ticket offers a more exclusive experience, including a vintage photo souvenir. The guided tour, available with an audioguide, is highly recommended to fully appreciate Gaudí's creative process and the symbolism within Casa Batlló.

Barcelona Nightlife

Barcelona, often called 'the city that never sleeps,' offers a night-life as diverse and vibrant as the city itself. Whether you're seeking trendy bars, live music venues, flamenco shows, or world-class nightclubs, Barcelona caters to every taste. The city's nightlife is not just about partying; it's a way of life, reflected in the locals' penchant for late-night dinners and gatherings.

Areas like the Gothic Quarter and El Born are packed with intimate tapas bars and traditional bodegas. Gracia, a bohemian neighborhood, is known for its live music venues and artisanal breweries. For a glamorous night out, head to the waterfront clubs in Port Olimpic. Flamenco lovers should not miss Tablao Cordobes in La Rambla, renowned for its authentic performances.

Remember, nightlife in Barcelona starts late and goes on until the early morning hours. Be prepared for late dinners (often after 9 PM) and even later clubbing. Dress code varies depending on the venue, but generally, Barcelonians dress stylishly for a night out. Always keep an eye on your belongings, especially in crowded places.

Day Trip to Montserrat

Just an hour's train ride from Barcelona, Montserrat is a serene mountain retreat, home to a Benedictine monastery and a revered statue of the Black Madonna, Catalonia's patron saint. This spiritual and cultural hub, nestled amidst rugged mountain peaks, offers a refreshing escape from the city bustle. Montserrat's unique setting and religious significance attract pilgrims and tourists alike.

Take a funicular or hike up the mountain to reach the monastery. Here, you can visit the basilica, see the Black Madonna, and enjoy the soul-stirring performance of the famed Montserrat Boys' Choir. The mountain's peak, accessible via a funicular, provides breathtaking views of the surrounding landscape.

Getting to Montserrat is straightforward, with regular trains from Barcelona's Plaça d'Espanya station. Once there, the rack railway or cable car can transport you to the monastery. To avoid crowds, aim to visit on weekdays and arrive early in the morning. Besides the monastery, Montserrat Natural Park offers excellent hiking trails, ranging from easy to challenging, rewarding you with stunning panoramic vistas.

Camp Nou

As the home of FC Barcelona, one of the world's most successful football clubs, Camp Nou is more than just a stadium. It's a pilgrimage site for football fans, boasting a rich history and an electrifying atmosphere. With a seating capacity of nearly 100,000, it's the largest stadium in Europe, echoing with chants, cheers, and the spirit of competition during match days.

The Camp Nou Experience, a tour of the stadium and its museum, is a must for football enthusiasts. The tour includes access to the players' tunnel, the pitch, the press room, and the commentary boxes. The museum showcases a fascinating collection of trophies, memorabilia, and interactive exhibits about the club's history.

Whether you're an FC Barcelona fan or not, experiencing a live match at Camp Nou can be thrilling. If this isn't possible, the stadium tour and museum visit are available all year round. Book your tickets online in advance to secure your spot. Don't forget to visit the FC Barcelona store for souvenirs and football merchandise.

Barcelona Cuisine

A gastronomic hub, Barcelona presents a culinary mosaic where traditional Catalan cooking meets innovative gourmet trends. The city's food scene is as diverse and colorful as its culture, featuring an array of seafood, locally grown produce, and regional wines. Barcelona's culinary landscape ranges from quaint tapas bars and market stalls to Michelin-starred establishments.

Seafood is an integral part of Barcelona's cuisine. Feast on dishes like paella, a flavorful rice dish with seafood, and fideuà, a similar dish made with noodles. Tapas, small plates meant for sharing, can be found all over the city. Popular tapas include patatas bravas (spicy potatoes), gambas al ajillo (garlic shrimp), and pimientos de padrón (fried green peppers).

For dessert, don't miss out on trying crema catalana, Catalonia's version of crème brûlée. Wine enthusiasts will appreciate Barcelona's proximity to several prominent wine regions, including Penedès and Priorat. For a local drink, try vermut, a fortified wine often served as an aperitif.

Culinary experiences in Barcelona extend beyond dining. Visit La Boqueria Market on La Rambla to experience the city's vibrant food culture. Join a cooking class or a food tour to learn more about Barcelona's gastronomy. Remember, dining in Barcelona is a leisurely experience, so take your time to savor the food and enjoy the convivial atmosphere.

Final Thoughts

Barcelona, an enchanting city where creativity blossoms, is full of surprises at every corner. With its stunning architecture, vibrant arts scene, and mouth-watering cuisine, the city promises an unforgettable experience for all who visit. As we conclude this chapter, let's touch upon some final tips and hidden gems to ensure your Barcelona trip is truly remarkable.

The city's excellent public transport makes getting around easy and convenient. The T10 ticket offers ten rides on buses, trams, and metro and is a cost-effective option for travelers. Barcelona is also a bike-friendly city, with numerous bike rental services and designated cycle paths.

Venture beyond the touristy areas and explore the lesser-known neighborhoods like Poblenou, known for its industrial heritage, arts scene, and the Rambla de Poblenou, a quieter alternative to La Rambla. For a unique shopping experience, visit the Encants Flea Market, one of the oldest markets in Europe, where you can find everything from antiques to second-hand goods.

While Barcelona's major sights are truly worth visiting, don't forget to take the time to simply wander around, soak up the atmosphere, and enjoy the city's rhythm. From the lively festivals and cultural events to tranquil parks and beautiful sunsets at the beach, there's much to love about Barcelona.

As we say goodbye to Barcelona and look forward to the next chapters of our Spanish journey, remember that travel is more than just visiting places. It's about immersing ourselves in the local culture, connecting with people, and creating memories that last a lifetime. So, here's to Barcelona, and here's to the adventures that await in Spain!

CHAPTER 3:
Seville
· · · · · · · · · · ·

The charm of Spain's Andalusian region is encapsulated by its vibrant capital, Seville, a city that marries the grandeur of a rich historical past with the irresistible allure of flamenco, fiestas, and a zestful food culture. Unfolding at the banks of the Guadalquivir River, Seville is a testament to Spain's complex history, adorned by architectural gems from the Moorish, Gothic, and Renaissance eras. Wrapped in the radiance of the sun and veiled in the aroma of blooming orange trees, Seville is a sensory delight.

Seville's storied past is a tale of civilizations, each of which left indelible imprints on its landscape and character. The Moors, who ruled here for over 500 years, constructed magnificent palaces and fortresses that today serve as picturesque reminders of a bygone era. The Christians, too, contributed immensely, creating awe-inspiring cathedrals and plazas. This intricate dance between Moorish and Christian cultures has created a city that feels like an open-air museum, full of tales waiting to be discovered.

Seville's soulful energy is magnified by the captivating rhythm of flamenco, a musical tradition originating from the Andalusian region. This deeply emotional dance form echoes in the city's ancient walls, infusing life into its cobblestone streets. From flamenco tablaos (venues) in the traditional Triana district to impromptu street performances, the passion of flamenco permeates Seville's atmosphere, creating a bond that connects locals and visitors alike.

Beyond its historical treasures and cultural richness, Seville also surprises with its flair for the avant-garde. It's a city where the cutting-edge architecture of structures like Metropol Parasol seamlessly merges with the ancient landmarks, projecting a cityscape that's as varied as it's intriguing. Seville isn't trapped in its past; it uses its history as a stepping stone towards a progressive future.

Of course, a journey through Seville isn't complete without indulging in its delectable cuisine. The city is a gastronomic paradise, where traditional Andalusian flavors meld with innovative culinary techniques. Whether it's savoring tapas at a bustling local market or dining at a chic rooftop restaurant overlooking the city, every meal in Seville is an event to be celebrated. Unraveling the charm of Seville means surrendering to its rhythm — basking in its sunshine, strolling through its historic quarters, swaying to the rhythm of flamenco, and savoring its culinary delights. As we delve into the marvels of Seville in this chapter, prepare to be enchanted by the splendors that this Andalusian gem has to offer. So, let's embark on this journey, for Seville awaits!

The Alcázar

Standing regally in the heart of Seville, the Alcázar is a palatial fortress and a shining example of Mudejar architecture, a unique style that blends Moorish and Christian design principles. The UNESCO World Heritage Site, whose foundations date back to the 10th century, is an intriguing labyrinth of ornate rooms, tranquil courtyards, and verdant gardens. As you navigate through the complex, the intricate tilework, arched doorways, and elegant stucco work reveal a fascinating blend of cultures.

In the Alcázar, every corner tells a story of Seville's multi-layered past. The Patio de las Doncellas, with its reflective water features, and the Salón de Embajadores, or Hall of Ambassadors, with its spectacular domed ceiling, are especially memorable. Outside, the lush gardens, dotted with fountains, pools, and pavilions, offer a serene retreat from the city's bustle.

When visiting, it's worth taking an audio guide or a guided tour to fully understand the history and significance of this incredible complex. Be sure to book your tickets online in advance, as the Alcázar is a popular attraction, and lines can be long. Also, remember to take time to soak in the peaceful atmosphere of the gardens.

Seville Cathedral and Giralda

The Seville Cathedral, or Cathedral of Saint Mary of the See, is not only the largest Gothic cathedral in the world but also an architectural marvel steeped in history. This colossal structure impresses with its soaring ceilings, intricate stone carvings, and priceless artworks. Perhaps the most iconic feature of the cathedral is La Giralda, a former minaret turned bell tower, which provides stunning panoramic views of the city.

Inside the cathedral, the vast nave, the ornate altarpiece, and the tomb of Christopher Columbus are not to be missed. Climbing La Giralda, an experience made easier by the absence of stairs in favor of a ramp, rewards you with breathtaking views of Seville's rooftops and beyond.

Remember to dress modestly when visiting the Seville Cathedral, as it is an active place of worship. An audio guide is available and recommended to appreciate the historical and artistic details of the cathedral fully. Plan your visit early in the day or late in the afternoon to avoid crowds, and don't forget your camera to capture the remarkable architectural features.

Plaza de España

Designed for the Ibero-American Exposition of 1929, Plaza de España is a striking semi-circular complex combining Renaissance and Moorish styles. The plaza, with its ornate bridges over a canal, beautifully tiled alcoves, and a towering central fountain, is a feast for the eyes. It's surrounded by Maria Luisa Park, providing a lush backdrop to this architectural spectacle.
Each alcove at the plaza represents a different province of Spain, adorned with colorful tilework depicting historical scenes. These alcoves make for great photo opportunities. The canal offers boat rentals, and the building houses some government offices and a museum.
Visiting the Plaza de España is free, and it's a great place to relax, enjoy a picnic, or take a leisurely boat ride on the canal. It can be particularly enchanting in the evening when the buildings are illuminated. Don't miss the opportunity to wander around Maria Luisa Park while you're in the area.

Triana District

Triana, located on the west bank of the Guadalquivir River, is a vibrant neighborhood with a unique identity. Known as the cradle of flamenco, it's a place where music, dance, and tradition thrive in every corner. Triana's past as a potter's quarter is still visible in the colorful ceramic tiles adorning its streets and buildings, adding a distinctive touch to the district.

A stroll through Triana's atmospheric streets reveals charming squares, lively markets, and historic churches. A visit to the Casa de la Memoria or the Flamenco Dance Museum offers a deep insight into the passionate world of flamenco, with exhibits and live performances. Don't miss the Mercado de Triana, a bustling food market, where you can sample local delicacies.

When in Triana, make sure to catch a live flamenco show for an authentic Andalusian experience. Enjoy a meal at one of the traditional tapas bars, and take a walk along Calle Betis for a picturesque view of the Seville skyline. Remember, Triana is best explored on foot, so wear comfortable shoes.

Metropol Parasol

In stark contrast to Seville's historic landmarks stands Metropol Parasol, a contemporary structure that has become a symbol of the city's modern face. Known locally as "Las Setas" (The Mushrooms) due to its distinctive shape, this wooden structure is one of the world's largest and offers panoramic views of the city from its walkways.

Beneath the parasol, you'll find the Antiquarium, a museum displaying Roman and Moorish artifacts discovered during the construction of the site. The structure itself houses a market, several bars and restaurants, and an elevated plaza for events.

Visit Metropol Parasol during the day to explore the Antiquarium and enjoy a meal in the market. However, don't miss the opportunity to ascend to the walkway at sunset. The golden light falling on the city offers an unforgettable view. There is a small fee to access the walkway, but it includes a drink at the rooftop bar.

María Luisa Park

María Luisa Park is Seville's principal green space, offering a tranquil escape from the urban hustle. This expansive park, designed in a mix of Moorish and English garden styles, is a haven of shady avenues, picturesque plazas, and vibrant flower beds. From playful fountains to exotic birds, it's a place full of delightful surprises.

The park houses several landmarks, including the grand Plaza de España, the charming Plaza de América, and the Museum of Popular Arts and Traditions. Whether you're enjoying a leisurely stroll, a romantic boat ride on the park's small canal, or a picnic under the trees, María Luisa Park is a refreshing retreat.

María Luisa Park is always open and free to enter, making it a great place for an early morning jog or a late-night walk. Renting a rowboat in the Plaza de España's canal can be a fun activity, and don't miss the opportunity to admire the beautiful tile work in the plazas. The park is also a perfect place for bird-watching, with many peacocks and ducks calling it home.

Seville Bullring

The Real Maestranza de Caballería de Sevilla, known simply as the Seville Bullring, is one of the most important and historic bullrings in Spain. This colossal circular structure, with its Baroque façade and impressive arena, is more than just a venue for bullfighting; it's a testament to a deeply-rooted tradition that remains a part of Spanish culture.

Inside, the Bullfighting Museum offers a compelling exploration of the history and evolution of bullfighting, showcasing a collection of costumes, photographs, and paintings. A guided tour of the arena and the stables provides an insightful look at the complexities of this controversial sport.

When planning a visit to the Seville Bullring, consider the cultural significance of bullfighting in Spain. While it may not appeal to everyone, the architectural grandeur and historical importance of the venue are undeniable. Guided tours are offered daily and provide a comprehensive overview of the site. If you choose to attend a bullfight, ensure you understand the nature of the event and its associated traditions.

Day Trip to Jerez

Less than an hour's drive from Seville, Jerez de la Frontera offers a delightful excursion. This charming city is renowned for its horse culture, flamenco music, and sherry wine production, representing the quintessence of Andalusian tradition.

Jerez is home to the Royal Andalusian School of Equestrian Art, a prestigious institution where you can watch spectacular horse shows. Also worth visiting is the Alcazar of Jerez, a Moorish fortress with beautiful gardens and a camera obscura. As for flamenco, several peñas (clubs) offer intimate performances, offering an authentic local experience.

When visiting Jerez, a tasting tour of a sherry bodega is a must, as this city is the birthplace of this famous fortified wine. Try to time your visit with a horse show at the Equestrian School, and enjoy an evening of flamenco for a truly Andalusian day out. Public transport between Seville and Jerez is frequent and convenient, but consider renting a car if you wish to explore the surrounding wine country.

Flamenco Show

Flamenco, a vibrant blend of song, dance, and guitar, is the heartbeat of Andalusian culture. This passionate and powerful art form, recognized as an Intangible Cultural Heritage by UNESCO, can be experienced in Seville's numerous tablaos (flamenco venues). A flamenco show, with its raw emotion and rhythmic intensity, is an experience that touches the soul.

Seville's flamenco scene is diverse, with performances ranging from intimate shows in small bars to larger productions in dedicated tablaos. Some venues also offer a dinner option, allowing you to savor local cuisine as you enjoy the performance. Among the popular spots are Casa de la Guitarra, Los Gallos, and El Palacio Andaluz.

When choosing a flamenco show, look for one that emphasizes authenticity over spectacle. Smaller venues often provide a more intimate and genuine experience. Although there are shows available throughout the day, a late-night performance is usually more atmospheric. Remember, flamenco is not just a show, but a profound expression of Andalusian identity – a window into the soul of Spain's southern region.

Torre del Oro

The Torre del Oro (Golden Tower), a dodecagonal military watchtower, stands majestically on the bank of the Guadalquivir River, its golden reflection shimmering in the water. Built in the early 13th century during the Almohad dynasty, the tower has served various functions over the centuries, from a defensive structure to a prison and even a safe for precious metals, hence its name.

Today, the Torre del Oro houses a small maritime museum that showcases Seville's rich naval history, featuring maps, compasses, models of old ships, and historical documents. The rooftop of the tower offers panoramic views over the Guadalquivir River and the cityscape, a sight particularly enchanting at sunset.

Visiting the Torre del Oro is a great way to delve into the maritime history of Seville. The views from the top are well worth the climb, especially on clear days. Try to plan your visit for late afternoon to enjoy a beautiful sunset from the rooftop. The entrance to the tower is free on Mondays, but it can get quite crowded.

Seville Cuisine

Seville's culinary scene is a glorious fusion of traditional Andalusian flavors and innovative gastronomic techniques. From the bustling food markets to the rustic tapas bars and gourmet restaurants, every corner of the city promises a culinary delight that is as colorful and vibrant as Seville itself.

Tapas, small savory dishes often enjoyed with a glass of local wine, are at the heart of Sevillian cuisine. Favorites include patatas bravas (spicy potatoes), espinacas con garbanzos (spinach with chickpeas), salmorejo (a cold tomato and bread soup), and montadito de pringá (a small sandwich filled with slow-cooked meat).

For a truly local experience, visit a neighborhood food market such as the Mercado de Triana or Mercado de Feria. Here, you can explore a variety of fresh produce, seafood, and local specialties. Don't miss out on tasting a glass of sherry or manzanilla, fortified wines native to the Andalusian region.

While in Seville, venture into a traditional tapas bar, where you can immerse yourself in the local dining culture. Be adventurous and try a variety of dishes. For seafood lovers, fried calamari, gambas al ajillo (garlic shrimp), and boquerones en vinagre (anchovies in vinegar) are must-try tapas. Pair your meal with a glass of local wine or a refreshing tinto de verano, a popular summer drink made with red wine and soda.

Final Thoughts

Seville, with its vibrant culture, magnificent architecture, and warm, inviting people, is a city that enchants and inspires. Each corner of this Andalusian gem reveals a new surprise, a new story, a new melody that lingers in the heart long after the journey ends.

When planning your visit, remember to take time to wander through the narrow, winding streets of the city's old quarters, such as the Santa Cruz or Arenal district, where the authentic charm of Seville truly shines. The city's numerous churches, like the Church of El Salvador or the Basilica of La Macarena, are also worth visiting for their artistic and historical significance.

Keep in mind that Seville, like much of Spain, operates on a different schedule than most European cities. Many shops close in the afternoon for siesta, and dinner often doesn't start until 9 p.m. or later. Embrace this relaxed pace and take the opportunity to enjoy a leisurely afternoon stroll or a relaxing break at a café.

Don't forget to venture outside the city center. The nearby town of Carmona offers a glimpse into a more rural Andalusian life, and the ancient city of Itálica, with its well-preserved Roman ruins, is just a short trip away.

As you prepare to say adiós to Seville, the memories of vibrant flamenco performances, sun-drenched plazas, fragrant orange trees, and mouth-watering tapas will no doubt fill your heart with longing for your next visit. Seville is not just a destination; it is a feeling, a celebration of life's simple pleasures, a melody that calls you back time and again.

So, hasta luego, Seville. We will dance again soon in the shadow of the Giralda, under the Andalusian sun.

CHAPTER 4:
Valencia
. . . .

Valencia, Spain's third-largest city, nestled on the country's eastern coastline, is a captivating fusion of ancient traditions and contemporary creativity. The birthplace of the famous paella, Valencia, seamlessly blends a rich cultural heritage with ground-breaking architecture and a vibrant gastronomic scene. It's a city where you can walk through the narrow, medieval streets of the Barrio del Carmen one moment and marvel at futuristic buildings in the City of Arts and Sciences the next. This dynamic juxtaposition is what makes Valencia a truly unique destination, offering diverse experiences to its visitors.

Valencia's rich history is palpable throughout the city. Its origins date back to 138 BC, when it was founded as a Roman colony. The legacy of the various civilizations that have called Valencia home – Romans, Visigoths, Moors, and Christians – is reflected in its rich architectural tapestry. From the impressive Valencia Cathedral, which houses the Holy Grail, to the Silk Exchange, a masterpiece of Gothic civil architecture, the city's monuments and buildings tell fascinating tales of a storied past.

But Valencia is not just about its historical legacy. It is a city that has embraced innovation and modernity with open arms. The City of Arts and Sciences, a futuristic complex of museums, theaters, and other cultural venues, is a testament to Valencia's commitment to cutting-edge architecture and design. The city's transformed riverbed, now a magnificent park that snakes through the urban landscape, reflects its innovative approach to urban planning.

The soul of Valencia, however, lies in its vibrant traditions and festivals. The Fallas Festival, a unique celebration filled with monumental sculptures, fireworks, and parades, is a spectacle that fills the city with energy and color each March. Equally captivating is the city's culinary culture. Valencia is the birthplace of paella, Spain's most famous dish, and exploring its food markets and tapas bars is a gastronomic adventure.

Beyond the city limits, the natural beauty of the Valencian community beckons. The Albufera Natural Park, home to the largest lake in Spain and a haven for diverse bird species, is a must-visit for nature lovers. Likewise, the beautiful beaches of the Costa Blanca and charming towns like Altea are just a short trip away.

Whether it's the allure of historical treasures, the excitement of contemporary architecture, the joy of lively festivals, the temptation of gastronomic delights, or the call of nature, Valencia has something to enchant everyone. So, let's embark on this journey to discover Valencia, where the old coexists with the new in a beautiful symphony.

City of Arts and Sciences

The City of Arts and Sciences, or Ciutat de les Arts i les Ciències, is a dazzling cultural complex that embodies Valencia's innovative spirit. The brainchild of renowned architect Santiago Calatrava, it's a collection of futuristic buildings that seem more like sculptures than edifices, spread over an area equivalent to 40 football fields. The complex includes the Hemisfèric (an IMAX cinema and digital planetarium), the Príncipe Felipe Science Museum, and the Palau de les Arts Reina Sofia (an opera house and performing arts center), among other attractions.

As you explore the site, you'll be fascinated by the fluidity of Calatrava's designs, which draw inspiration from natural forms such as the human eye and the skeleton of a whale. The structures, surrounded by turquoise pools of water, offer an arresting spectacle, especially when illuminated at night. Whether you're keen on opera, interested in science, or simply a fan of extraordinary architecture, the City of Arts and Sciences offers a unique cultural experience.

Consider purchasing a combined ticket if you plan to visit more than one venue. Evenings offer an enchanting atmosphere, with the buildings lit up against the night sky. And don't forget to capture some photographs; the complex is one of the most photographed sites in Valencia.

Valencia Cathedral

Standing proudly in the heart of Valencia, the Valencia Cathedral is a testament to the city's rich architectural heritage. Built between the 13th and 15th centuries, the cathedral showcases a harmonious blend of styles, from Romanesque and Gothic to Baroque. The cathedral's most remarkable treasure is the Santo Cáliz, believed by many to be the Holy Grail.

The Cathedral's interior is equally captivating, with its beautiful frescoes, stained glass windows, and intricate carvings. The octagonal bell tower, El Miguelete, offers panoramic views over the city for those willing to climb its 207 steps. Don't miss the stunning golden Basilica of the Virgin located next to the cathedral, home to the revered image of the Virgin Mary.

To fully appreciate the Cathedral's historical and religious significance, consider hiring an audio guide or joining a guided tour. Remember to dress respectfully when visiting. Climbing the Miguelete Tower is a must for the stunning views it offers, but be prepared for a steep ascent.

Central Market

Valencia's Central Market, or Mercado Central, is a food lover's paradise. Housed in a stunning Modernist building adorned with ceramic tiles, glass, and iron, the market is one of the largest in Europe. Here, over 900 stalls display an array of fresh produce, from fruits, vegetables, and meats to cheeses, spices, and an impressive array of seafood.

As you wander through the bustling aisles, you'll be drawn in by the vibrant colors and enticing aromas. It's the perfect place to sample local products like jamón ibérico, Valencian oranges, or horchata, a traditional drink made from tigernuts. For a more in-depth experience, look for a cooking class that includes a tour of the market.

The market is open from Monday to Saturday, and it's best to arrive early to avoid crowds and to find the freshest produce. Don't forget to check out the market's Art Nouveau architecture, especially the beautiful stained glass and mosaics. And remember, it's not just about buying; engaging with the friendly vendors is part of the experience.

Turia Gardens

Turia Gardens is an urban oasis that stretches for about nine kilometers across Valencia. The park, set in the former riverbed of the Turia River, is the perfect place to escape the city's hustle and bustle. Here, locals and tourists alike enjoy cycling, running, or simply relaxing under the shade of lush trees. The park also houses several cultural and recreational attractions, including the City of Arts and Sciences and the Gulliver Park, a playground based on the tale of Gulliver's Travels.

The gardens are a testament to creative urban planning. They feature beautifully landscaped sections with palm trees, fragrant orange groves, and rose gardens. Sculptures, fountains, and bridges add to the park's charm. The park is also home to a multitude of bird species, making it a haven for birdwatchers.

Turia Gardens are open all day and night, providing a safe and enjoyable place for a leisurely walk or bike ride at any time. Bike rentals are available at various points along the park. Don't forget to visit the Palau de la Música, a concert hall located in the gardens with a beautiful glass dome.

La Lonja de la Seda

The Lonja de la Seda, or Silk Exchange, is one of the most iconic monuments in Valencia and a UNESCO World Heritage site. Built in the late 15th century, the Lonja is a symbol of Valencia's golden age when it was a major center for silk trade. With its soaring Gothic arches and intricate stone carvings, the building is an outstanding example of secular Gothic architecture.

Inside, the main attraction is the Sala de Contratación, or Contract Hall, with its forest of twisted columns stretching towards the ribbed vaulted ceiling. Upstairs, you can visit the Consulado del Mar, where a stunning wooden ceiling showcases Renaissance art. The Lonja's Patio de los Naranjos, a courtyard filled with orange trees, offers a serene spot to soak up the atmosphere. The Lonja de la Seda is open daily, and entrance is free on Sundays. An audio guide is available for those wishing to delve into the history of the Silk Exchange. Don't forget to admire the facade's carvings, which include a variety of curious and grotesque figures.

Bioparc Valencia

Bioparc Valencia represents a new concept in zoo design, where visitors can observe animals in as close to their natural habitats as possible, without visible barriers. Located at the western end of Turia Gardens, the park spreads over 10 hectares and recreates the landscapes of Africa, from the Savannah to Madagascar. The park is home to a wide array of species, including gorillas, leopards, rhinos, giraffes, and lemurs, many of them participating in European conservation programs. Thanks to the zoo-immersion concept, you can watch these animals up close, separated only by streams, ponds, or rocks. The park also offers daily feeding talks, where you can learn more about the animals from the keepers.

Plan at least half a day to fully enjoy the Bioparc experience. The park is less crowded on weekdays or early in the morning, which is also a good time to observe animals as they're most active. Remember to wear comfortable shoes, as there's a lot of walking involved.

The Albufera Natural Park

Albufera Natural Park, located just south of Valencia, is a paradise for nature lovers. Covering over 21,000 hectares, the park is home to the Albufera Lagoon, one of the largest and most important wetland areas in the Iberian Peninsula. Here, you can observe an abundance of bird species, making it a popular spot for birdwatching, especially during migration periods.

Visitors can enjoy a boat trip on the lagoon, walk along the trails, or visit the traditional fishing villages scattered around the park. The rice fields surrounding the lagoon create a distinctive landscape, especially during the growing season when the fields are flooded, creating a mirror effect with the sky.

Consider hiring a local guide to help spot and identify the many bird species that inhabit the park. Boat trips on the lagoon are a highlight and offer a unique perspective of the park. Also, don't miss out on trying a traditional Valencian paella, which gets its unique flavor from the rice grown in the fields of Albufera.

Day Trip to Altea

Nestled between the sea and mountains, Altea is a charming town that's perfect for a day trip from Valencia. Known for its whitewashed old town, blue-domed church, and beautiful sea views, Altea is often referred to as the crown jewel of Costa Blanca. Wander through the narrow, cobbled streets, admire the Mediterranean architecture, and take in the panoramic views from the Plaza de la Iglesia.

The town also boasts a thriving art scene, with numerous galleries and craft shops. The seafront promenade is lined with restaurants and cafes, making it the perfect place to unwind and enjoy local cuisine, with the Mediterranean Sea as your backdrop. Travel to Altea by train for a scenic journey along the coast. The old town is hilly, so wear comfortable shoes. Also, remember to check the schedule for the last train back to Valencia, as it can change depending on the season.

Fallas Museum

The Fallas Museum offers a glimpse into Valencia's most famous and extravagant festival, Las Fallas. Held annually in March, the festival sees the city filled with enormous, intricate sculptures ("fallas") that are eventually set ablaze. The museum houses a collection of "ninots" (figurines) that were saved from the flames, offering a fascinating look at the artistry and satire involved in their creation.

The displays, organized chronologically, allow visitors to trace the evolution of Fallas art over the decades. Besides the ninots, the museum also provides information about the festival's history, traditions, and the painstaking process of building the fallas. The Fallas Museum is a must-visit for anyone interested in Valencia's unique cultural heritage. Be sure to take advantage of the audio guides available, as they provide valuable context and anecdotes about the displays. Visit during Fallas season for the most immersive experience, but be prepared for larger crowds.

Valencia's Silk Exchange

The Silk Exchange, or "La Lonja de la Seda", is a magnificent example of late Gothic architecture. Built between 1482 and 1548, it was the center of Valencia's silk trade, which contributed significantly to the city's prosperity during the 15th and 16th centuries. Today, it stands as a symbol of the city's rich history and has been declared a UNESCO World Heritage Site.

Visitors can explore the grand Trading Hall, with its stunning spiral columns, the orange-tree-filled Patio, and the Consulate of the Sea, which once resolved maritime and trade disputes. The building's intricate stone carvings, reminiscent of medieval craftsmanship, are also a sight to behold.

A visit to La Lonja de la Seda is like stepping back in time. The detailed audioguide, available in multiple languages, provides interesting historical context. Try to visit in the morning or late afternoon when the sunlight beautifully illuminates the Trading Hall's column forest.

Valencia Cuisine

Valencia is the birthplace of Spain's most famous dish, paella. Valencian cuisine emphasizes fresh, local ingredients, and it's hard to get more authentic than a traditional Valencian paella. Unlike other variations, the original recipe includes rabbit, chicken, green beans, and butter beans, all cooked in a shallow pan over a wood fire.

Beyond paella, Valencia offers a diverse culinary scene. Other regional dishes to try include "fideuà" (a noodle-based dish similar to paella), "arroso al forn" (oven-baked rice), and "horchata" (a sweet drink made from tiger nuts) paired with "fartons" (elongated sugar-glazed pastries). Valencia's Central Market, one of the largest in Europe, is the perfect place to discover the region's fresh produce and gourmet products.

If you're a foodie with a sweet tooth, Valencia will not disappoint you. The city's pastry shops offer an array of traditional sweets, including "turron" (a type of nougat), "buñuelos" (deep-fried dough balls often eaten during the Fallas Festival), and "pasteles de boniato" (sweet potato pastries). Sampling these local treats is a must when in Valencia.

For those interested in diving deeper into Valencia's culinary culture, consider signing up for a cooking class. This is an excellent opportunity to learn how to prepare traditional dishes like paella under the guidance of local chefs. Not only will you gain a deeper appreciation for the region's cuisine, but you'll also acquire a new set of culinary skills to take home with you.

When in Valencia, eating paella by the sea is a must-do. Remember that traditional Valencian paella is usually served at lunchtime, and it's common for restaurants to require orders for a minimum of two people. Also, the local custom is to eat paella straight from the pan!

Final Thoughts

Valencia is a city that expertly balances the past with the future. From the futuristic City of Arts and Sciences to the historic Silk Exchange, it offers an intriguing blend of sights that cater to a wide range of interests. Take a leisurely stroll in the extensive Turia Gardens, relax on the city's beautiful beaches, or immerse yourself in the local culture by visiting the bustling Central Market and the Fallas Museum.

Although Valencia may not be as internationally famous as Madrid or Barcelona, it offers an authentic Spanish experience. The city has a unique rhythm of life, from its leisurely afternoon "siestas" to its vibrant nightlife. Its traditions, such as the Fallas Festival and the ubiquitous paella, provide visitors with an intimate glimpse into the Valencian way of life.

In addition to the highlights covered in this chapter, the city offers numerous other attractions. The Oceanogràfic, part of the City of Arts and Sciences complex, is Europe's largest aquarium and home to over 500 different species. For art lovers, the Valencian Institute of Modern Art hosts an excellent collection of 20th-century Spanish art. History enthusiasts shouldn't miss the Torres de Quart and Torres de Serranos, two impressive Gothic city gates that once formed part of Valencia's city wall. Ultimately, Valencia is a city that invites exploration and rewards curiosity. Its mix of history, culture, cuisine, and innovative design makes it a must-visit destination for any travel enthusiast. From its sun-soaked beaches to its ancient winding streets, Valencia offers a myriad of experiences just waiting to be discovered. No matter how long you stay, you'll leave with a piece of this magical city in your heart and a desire to return to uncover more of its secrets. Valencia truly is a hidden gem, representing the best of Spain and all its captivating allure.

CHAPTER 5:
Bilbao

· · · · · · · · · · ·

Nestled in the heart of Spain's Basque Country, the city of Bilbao offers a rich blend of old-world charm, cutting-edge architecture, and a lively cultural scene. Once a major industrial centre, Bilbao has evolved over the years into an exciting, modern city known for its innovative spirit and vibrant atmosphere.

Visitors to Bilbao are met with a dazzling array of experiences. As you wander through the city, you'll find yourself immersed in its remarkable transformation. From the historical Casco Viejo (Old Town) with its narrow, winding streets and picturesque plazas, to the ultramodern Guggenheim Museum, which has become a symbol of the city's regeneration, there's a delightful surprise around every corner.

One of Bilbao's defining features is its commitment to art and culture. The Guggenheim Museum, with its bold, futuristic design and impressive contemporary art collection, is a testament to this. However, art in Bilbao is not confined to the walls of its galleries. Public art installations and creative architectural designs can be found throughout the city, turning a casual stroll into an open-air museum tour.

However, there's more to Bilbao than its arts scene. The city is also a foodie's paradise, renowned for its culinary tradition. From pintxos bars serving up bite-sized Basque delights to Michelin-starred restaurants offering gastronomic experiences, the city's food culture is as diverse and dynamic as its architecture.

Bilbao's location, surrounded by green rolling hills and close to the sea, provides a beautiful backdrop to the cityscape. It also offers plenty of opportunities for outdoor activities, from leisurely walks along the Nervión river to adventurous hikes in the nearby mountains. For a refreshing escape from the city, consider a day trip to the stunning Gaztelugatxe island, just a short drive away.

Embracing both tradition and innovation, Bilbao represents the best of the Basque Country. With its rich history, dynamic arts scene, delectable cuisine, and friendly locals, the city provides an unforgettable travel experience. This guide will take you on a journey through Bilbao's must-see attractions, its hidden gems, and the tastes and sounds that give the city its unique character. Welcome to Bilbao, the revitalised city of the Basque Country.

Guggenheim Museum

The Guggenheim Museum is a must-visit for any art and architecture lover. Designed by renowned architect Frank Gehry, its shimmering, curved exterior, covered in titanium plates, is a sight to behold and has become an icon of modern architecture. The museum stands as a symbol of Bilbao's transformation from an industrial port city to a hub of contemporary art and culture.

Inside, the Guggenheim Museum houses an extensive collection of contemporary art, featuring works from international artists such as Jeff Koons and Anish Kapoor. The museum's permanent collection is complimented by a rotating series of temporary exhibitions, which further enrich the artistic offering.

The museum itself, with its soaring atrium and interconnecting spaces, offers an immersive and exploratory experience.

Visitors are encouraged to explore the exterior spaces of the museum as well, which hosts several installations, including Jeff Koons' famous "Puppy", a towering terrier covered in flowering plants. The Guggenheim offers free entrance on select dates and times, and it's recommended to book your tickets in advance, particularly during peak seasons.

Casco Viejo

The Casco Viejo, also known as the "Seven Streets," is the historical heart of Bilbao. Its labyrinth of narrow streets, filled with beautifully preserved traditional Basque architecture, offers a striking contrast to the modern structures of the new city. Casco Viejo is rich in history, character, and local life, making it a captivating area to explore.

Here, you'll find the city's original cathedral, Santiago Cathedral, and numerous other historical landmarks. The streets are teeming with a variety of shops, from local artisan boutiques to more well-known Spanish brands. Casco Viejo is also home to the bustling Ribera Market, one of the largest covered markets in Europe.

The evenings bring a vibrant atmosphere to the quarter, as the streets fill with locals enjoying pintxos (small snacks) and drinks in the many bars and restaurants. For a local experience, join the evening pintxos crawl or take part in a traditional Basque cider tasting.

Bilbao Fine Arts Museum

Offering a balance to the contemporary art at the Guggenheim, the Bilbao Fine Arts Museum showcases a collection spanning from the Middle Ages to the present. Its collection, considered one of the finest in Spain, comprises over 10,000 works including paintings, sculptures, drawings, and applied arts.

The museum features works by significant Spanish artists such as El Greco, Zurbarán, Goya, and Sorolla, as well as notable Basque artists. Also, it hosts a collection of international art, with pieces from artists like Van Dyck, Gauguin, and Bacon.

The museum is located next to the Doña Casilda Iturrizar Park, making it a perfect stop during a leisurely walk. Free guided tours are offered in both Spanish and English, providing a deeper understanding of the artworks. Every Wednesday, the museum offers free admission, making it a great opportunity for budget-conscious travelers. However, the museum is often less crowded during regular weekdays.

Artxanda Funicular

A trip to Bilbao wouldn't be complete without a visit to the scenic viewpoint of Artxanda. Accessible via a charming century-old funicular railway, the summit of Mount Artxanda offers breathtaking panoramic views of Bilbao and its surrounding areas.

Once at the top, aside from the views, visitors can explore walking trails, gardens, and recreational areas. There are also several restaurants and a picnic area, making it an ideal spot for a leisurely lunch while enjoying the scenery. The viewpoint is especially popular at sunset, when the cityscape of Bilbao is bathed in a warm, golden glow.

The funicular station is just a short walk from the city center, making it an easily accessible excursion. It's recommended to purchase round-trip tickets in advance to avoid queues. Also, don't forget to bring a camera to capture the stunning views.

San Mamés Stadium

San Mamés Stadium, dubbed "The Cathedral" by locals, is more than just a sports venue; it's the beating heart of Bilbao's football culture. Home to Athletic Bilbao, one of Spain's oldest football clubs, the stadium holds a significant place in the city's identity and social life.

The stadium, with its impressive modern design, offers a capacity of over 53,000 seats and is known for its electrifying atmosphere during matches. Even if you're not a football fan, taking a guided tour of the stadium and its museum provides fascinating insights into the club's history and Basque football culture.

Tours are usually available on non-match days and include access to the pitch, changing rooms, and the press room. Tickets can be purchased in advance online or at the stadium. If your visit coincides with a match day, experiencing a game with the passionate local fans is an unforgettable experience.

Day Trip to Gaztelugatxe

Just a short drive from Bilbao, Gaztelugatxe is a natural wonder that captures the rugged beauty of the Basque Country's coastline. This small island, topped by a hermitage dedicated to John the Baptist, is connected to the mainland by a winding stone bridge and 241-step staircase.

Once at the top, visitors are rewarded with stunning views of the Cantabrian Sea and the surrounding cliffs. The site has gained international fame as a filming location for the television series "Game of Thrones", where it was featured as the fortress of Dragonstone.

Gaztelugatxe can be reached by car or public transport from Bilbao. It's recommended to wear comfortable shoes for the hike and to visit early in the morning or late in the afternoon to avoid crowds. After the climb, ringing the bell of the hermitage three times and making a wish is a local tradition not to be missed.

Plaza Nueva

Plaza Nueva, or New Square, is a quintessential meeting point in the heart of Bilbao's old town, Casco Viejo. This 19th-century Neoclassical square, framed by uniform arcaded buildings, is filled with shops, cafés, and restaurants, where locals and tourists alike come to enjoy pintxos and Basque sidra (cider).

Throughout the week, Plaza Nueva is a hub of activity, hosting a weekly Sunday market where collectors come to hunt for stamps, coins, and other curiosities. During local festivals, the square is often at the heart of the celebrations, brimming with music, traditional dances, and theatrical performances.

Venture to the plaza in the late afternoon or evening when it's buzzing with life. Many of the surrounding bars offer pintxo-pote, a local tradition of pairing a pintxo (a small snack) with a drink, usually on specific days of the week. It's a great way to sample local flavors and immerse yourself in the local culture.

Bilbao Riverside Walk

One of the best ways to appreciate Bilbao is by taking a leisurely walk along the banks of the Nervión River. This scenic route, stretching from the Old Town to the Guggenheim Museum, allows you to enjoy a mix of Bilbao's historic charm and modern architecture, all while taking in the lively riverfront atmosphere. Along the way, you'll pass by iconic landmarks such as the Arriaga Theatre, the City Hall, and the Bilbao Ribera Market, the largest covered market in Europe. You'll also have a chance to admire some of the city's impressive bridges, including the Zubizuri, a modern footbridge designed by architect Santiago Calatrava.

The riverside walk can be enjoyed at any time of the day, but is particularly atmospheric in the evening, when many of the buildings and bridges are beautifully illuminated. Keep in mind that the path is also bike-friendly, so consider renting a bicycle for a quicker tour of the area.

Azkuna Zentroa

Azkuna Zentroa, formerly known as Alhóndiga Bilbao, is a multi-purpose venue that perfectly embodies the innovative spirit of the city. Originally built as a wine warehouse in the early 20th century, the building was transformed into a vibrant cultural and leisure center by the renowned French designer Philippe Starck.

Today, Azkuna Zentroa offers a variety of spaces including a media library, exhibition halls, a fitness center, and a rooftop swimming pool with a transparent floor that allows visitors below to watch swimmers overhead. Its interior is remarkable

for its 43 uniquely designed columns, each representing different architectural styles and civilizations.

The center hosts a wide range of activities, from art exhibitions
and film screenings to workshops and fitness classes. Check
their event calendar in advance to see what's on. Don't miss
the opportunity to visit the rooftop, where you can enjoy a
swim with a unique view or relax at the café while admiring the
cityscape.

Bilbao's Bridges

Bilbao's urban landscape is characterized by the presence of
numerous bridges that cross the Nervión River, connecting
different parts of the city. These bridges are not just functional
structures; they are landmarks that each carry a piece of Bilbao's
history and architectural identity.

Among the most emblematic is the Zubizuri, or "White Bridge".
Designed by the world-renowned architect Santiago Calatrava,
the bridge is known for its distinctive arching design and glass-
tiled walkway. Equally noteworthy is the La Salve Bridge, an
older construction that gained a new look with a red gate addition, courtesy of French artist Daniel Buren, to celebrate the
10th anniversary of the Guggenheim Museum.

Other significant bridges include the Arenal Bridge, a beautifully preserved 19th-century iron bridge that connects the
Old Town with the Ensanche district, and the Deusto Bridge,
an elegant bascule bridge that has stood since the 1930s. For
a unique experience, visitors can also cross the Vizcaya Bridge,
the world's oldest transporter bridge and a UNESCO World
Heritage Site, via its gondola or the high-level walkway.

Bilbao Cuisine

The gastronomy of Bilbao is a celebration of the region's bounty and the Basque culinary tradition. At the heart of this are the pintxos, Basque Country's version of tapas, but often more intricate and innovative. These small bites are usually served atop a slice of bread, and range from traditional combinations such as cod and peppers to avant-garde creations that wouldn't be out of place in a gourmet restaurant.

Exploring the city's pintxos bars is an essential part of the Bilbao experience. Many establishments line the streets of the Casco Viejo and the Ensanche district, offering counters laden with an array of colourful pintxos. Tradition dictates that you stand at the bar while enjoying your pintxo, accompanied by a glass of txakoli, a slightly sparkling white wine typical of the region.

Beyond pintxos, Bilbao also offers high-end dining options with several Michelin-starred restaurants. Notable mentions include Azurmendi, where chef Eneko Atxa serves innovative dishes in an eco-friendly greenhouse, and Mina, which prides itself on its seasonally changing tasting menus. Another culinary highlight in Bilbao is the Mercado de la Ribera, a vibrant market where you can buy fresh local produce or enjoy cooked meals at the food stalls.

Bilbao's gastronomy also extends to its confectionery. Pastries like 'canutillos de Bilbao' filled with custard, and 'Bilbainitos', small cakes topped with nuts and glazed with apricot jam, are some local favourites you can find in the city's pastelerías. Remember, the secret to fully enjoying the culinary scene in Bilbao is to eat as the locals do: go 'pintxo-pote', hopping from bar to bar, tasting different dishes along the way.

Final Thoughts

Bilbao's transformation from a gritty industrial hub to a vibrant city of art, culture, and gastronomy is nothing short of remarkable. This metamorphosis is not only evident in the city's physical landscape, but also in the spirit of its people who are proud of their Basque heritage while embracing the new.

For visitors seeking more cultural insights, the Basque Museum provides an in-depth look at the Basque people's history and culture. Similarly, the Maritime Museum is an excellent place to understand the city's close relationship with the Nervión River and its maritime past.

While the city's revitalised centre and the Guggenheim often take centre stage, don't miss the chance to explore Bilbao's diverse neighbourhoods. From the bohemian vibe of the Bilbao la Vieja to the traditional ambiance of the Deusto district, each area offers a different perspective of Bilbao.

Bilbao also serves as an excellent base for exploring the Basque Country. Coastal cities like San Sebastián, known for its beautiful beaches and gastronomic scene, and smaller fishing towns like Lekeitio and Bermeo, are just a short drive away. Nearby, the UNESCO Biosphere Reserve of Urdaibai offers beautiful natural scenery and excellent bird watching opportunities.

As a visitor, embrace the Bilbao lifestyle. Take leisurely strolls along the riverside promenade, delve into the lively food scene, appreciate the architecture, and immerse yourself in the city's art and culture. Remember, Bilbao is more than just a city; it's an experience, a testament to resilience and reinvention, a place where tradition and innovation coexist harmoniously, a true industrial phoenix that has risen with even greater splendour. Make your own journey here, and let Bilbao leave an indelible mark in your traveller's heart.

CHAPTER 6:
Granada
. . . .

Nestled at the foot of the Sierra Nevada Mountains, in the autonomous region of Andalusia, lies Granada, a city that effortlessly weaves together threads of different cultures into a stunning tapestry. Home to the magnificent Alhambra Palace and the historic Arab quarter of Albayzín, Granada is a city where Moorish influence still echoes strong, complemented by a rich Christian heritage and a lively, contemporary spirit.

This city tells a tale of convergence, where two prominent cultures of history – Islam and Christianity – met and left their indelible marks. Centuries of coexistence have created an environment where intricate Islamic artisanship blends seamlessly with grandiose Christian architecture, creating a distinctive architectural landscape that holds the power to fascinate and inspire.

But Granada is more than just a visual treat; it's a city to be experienced with all senses. The aroma of exotic spices wafting from the Arab market, the distant strumming of a Spanish guitar that guides you through the narrow, winding alleyways of Albayzín, the chorus of birds that accompany a peaceful stroll through the Generalife gardens, or the taste of a traditional tapa enjoyed in a lively bar — these are the moments that define the Granada experience.

A significant part of Granada's charm also lies in its geographical diversity. From the snow-capped peaks of Sierra Nevada, where adventure seekers can indulge in winter sports, to the sunny Mediterranean beaches of Costa Tropical just an hour's drive away, Granada offers an array of natural landscapes that are as diverse as its cultural heritage.

And then, there is the city's vibrant modern life. With a large student population, Granada is always brimming with energy. Cafés, taverns, and tapas bars line the city streets, and the sound of flamenco rhythm regularly fills the night air. Street art, particularly in the district of Realejo, adds a touch of contemporary vibrancy to the city's historic backdrop.

A trip to Granada is like stepping into a beautifully written historical novel. Each monument, each street, and each square has a story to tell — tales of sultans and queens, of poets and artists, of conquests and reconquests. Yet, despite its deep connection to the past, Granada remains firmly rooted in the present. It's a city where history and modernity engage in a constant dance, creating an ambiance that is uniquely Granadan.

As you plan your journey to this enchanting Andalusian city, prepare to be captivated by its historical treasures, its natural beauty, its vibrant culture, and its warm, hospitable people. Granada is more than a destination; it's an experience that lingers in your memory long after your visit. So come and uncover the many facets of this Andalusian gem, and let the magic of Granada weave its spell on you.

The Alhambra

The Alhambra, often considered the crown jewel of Granada, is an impressive testament to the city's Moorish legacy. This majestic hilltop fortress and palace complex, whose name translates to "The Red One" due to its reddish walls, dates back to the 9th century. However, it was the Nasrid Dynasty in the 13th and 14th centuries that gave the Alhambra its most distinguished features: intricate geometric patterns, arabesques, and calligraphic inscriptions that embellish walls, ceilings, and arches, reflecting the pinnacle of Islamic art and architecture.

The complex includes the Nasrid Palaces, the Alcazaba fortress, and the Generalife gardens. Each part of the Alhambra reveals its own history and grandeur, with ornate courtyards like the Court of the Lions, panoramic viewpoints such as the Tower of the Princesses, and lush gardens radiating tranquillity.

Booking your tickets well in advance is highly recommended due to the Alhambra's popularity. Audioguides are available to enrich your visit with historical and architectural details. The view of the Alhambra illuminated at night, seen from the Mirador de San Nicolas in the Albayzín district, is a sight not to be missed.

Albayzín

Albayzín, Granada's old Arab quarter, is an enchanting maze of narrow winding streets, whitewashed houses, hidden squares, and stunning views. Recognized as a UNESCO World Heritage site, it's an area where Granada's Moorish past feels vividly alive. As you stroll along the cobblestone lanes, the scent of jasmine fills the air, and the sound of trickling water from hidden fountains completes the idyllic setting.

The district's highlight is the Mirador de San Nicolas, a viewpoint that offers a breathtaking panorama of the Alhambra against the backdrop of the Sierra Nevada mountains. Also, visit the historic El Bañuelo, an excellently preserved Arab bathhouse, and the ancient mosque that now serves as the Church of San Salvador.

Keep in mind that the streets of Albayzín are steep and can be a bit challenging to navigate. However, taking your time to explore, maybe stopping for a Moroccan tea or visiting one of the many artisanal shops, is part of the charm of this historic quarter.

Sacromonte

Perched above the city, adjacent to Albayzín, the Sacromonte district is known as the heartland of Granada's Roma (Gypsy) community and is famed for its unique cave dwellings and flamenco tradition. The caves, dug into the hillside, were initially inhabited by the Romani people in the 15th century and have since become synonymous with the district's identity.

Sacromonte is also recognized as the birthplace of the Zambra style of flamenco, an emotive dance filled with passionate rhythms and movements. Watching a live Zambra performance in one of the neighborhood's caves, like those in Cueva de La Rocío or Cueva del Sacromonte, is an unforgettable experience that perfectly encapsulates the district's rich cultural heritage.

Additionally, the Sacromonte Abbey offers stunning city views and houses important religious artifacts. Walking tours are an excellent way to explore and understand the district's history and cultural significance. Keep in mind that the area's terrain is hilly, so wear comfortable shoes and take your time to enjoy the views and atmosphere.

Granada Cathedral

A masterpiece of Spanish Renaissance architecture, the Granada Cathedral, also known as the Cathedral of the Incarnation, is a symbol of Christian influence in Granada. Constructed on the site of the city's main mosque after the Christian Reconquista, the cathedral took nearly two centuries to complete, resulting in an intriguing mix of architectural styles.

The grand façade of the cathedral will catch your eye, but it's the interior that truly mesmerizes. Vast, elegant, and filled with light, the cathedral's main chapel showcases an impressive collection of artwork, while the numerous side chapels each tell their own unique story. Notably, the cathedral houses a magnificent 18th-century organ, known for its historical significance and musical quality.

Guided tours are available to provide a deeper understanding of the cathedral's history and architectural details. Don't miss the opportunity to climb to the top of the cathedral for a panoramic view of the city. As the cathedral is a popular attraction, consider visiting early in the day to avoid crowds.

Royal Chapel of Granada

Adjacent to the Granada Cathedral, you'll find the Royal Chapel of Granada, a mausoleum that holds significant historical importance. It's here where Catholic Monarchs Ferdinand and Isabella, the rulers responsible for the Reconquista that ended Moorish rule in Spain, are laid to rest.

The chapel is an exemplary piece of Gothic architecture, with its stunning vaulted ceiling and detailed stained-glass windows. The main attraction, however, is the marble tombs of the

Catholic Monarchs and their successors, which are beautifully sculpted and surrounded by intricate ironwork. Also, don't miss the small museum within the chapel that exhibits a collection of royal artefacts, including Queen Isabella's personal art collection and Ferdinand's sword.

Remember to dress respectfully when visiting this active place of worship. Guided tours are available and highly recommended to fully appreciate the historical and cultural significance of the Royal Chapel.

Day Trip to Sierra Nevada

For those seeking a respite from the city's cultural landmarks, a day trip to the Sierra Nevada offers a different kind of spectacle. This mountain range, whose name means "Snowy Range" in Spanish, is home to Spain's highest peak, Mulhacén, and provides a stunning backdrop to the city of Granada.

During the winter, the Sierra Nevada becomes a popular skiing destination, with a variety of slopes suitable for both beginners and experienced skiers. In the summer months, the mountains transform into a haven for hikers, with trails that offer breathtaking views over Andalusia. You can also visit the Sierra Nevada National Park, a biodiversity hotspot that hosts numerous endemic species.

To reach the Sierra Nevada, you can opt for public transportation, car hire, or organized tours. For skiing or hiking, it's essential to check the weather conditions beforehand and prepare accordingly. And no matter the season, don't forget to bring a camera to capture the unforgettable vistas that the Sierra Nevada provides.

Generalife

Located adjacent to the Alhambra, the Generalife serves as a tranquil oasis away from the city bustle. This picturesque estate was the leisure place of the Nasrid kings of Granada, providing a cool respite from the Andalusian heat. Comprising lush gardens, ornamental fountains, and elegant pavilions, the Generalife offers a serene escape where nature and architecture blend harmoniously.

The key attractions include the Patio de la Acequia, a long pool flanked by flower beds, fountains, and myrtle hedges, and the Patio de la Sultana, known for its ancient cypress tree linked to a romantic legend. Each corner of Generalife is imbued with a sense of tranquility, enhanced by the ambient sound of trickling water.

To avoid the crowds, consider visiting early in the morning or late in the afternoon. Your Alhambra ticket will include access to the Generalife, but remember to adhere to your allocated time slot.

Granada's Street Art

While Granada's history is etched into its ancient buildings, the city's vibrant street art scene offers a modern contrast. Much of this work is concentrated in the Realejo and Albayzín districts, where walls, shutters, and underpasses have become canvases for local and international artists.

Granada's most famous street artist is Raúl Ruiz, known as 'El Niño de las Pinturas'. His thought-provoking murals, often featuring children and elderly people coupled with poetic phrases, have become emblematic of the city's street art scene. Each piece is a statement, reflecting on society, philosophy, or local culture. You can explore Granada's street art on your own, or join a guided street art tour to gain deeper insights into the artists and their work. Either way, keep your camera at the ready, as these striking artworks make for excellent photo opportunities.

Hammam Al Ándalus

Step into Hammam Al Ándalus, and you'll be transported back in time to the days of Al-Andalus. This traditional Arab bath, situated at the foot of the Alhambra, provides a unique opportunity to immerse yourself in Andalusian history while indulging in a soothing spa experience.

The Hammam is a labyrinth of vaulted rooms, each filled with pools of varying temperatures. The ritual involves moving between these pools, from the warm bath to the hot bath, then cooling off in the cold bath, before finally resting in the relaxation room. There's also the option to receive a traditional kessa massage, which will leave your skin feeling incredibly smooth.

Booking in advance is highly recommended as the Hammam can fill up quickly. Remember to bring your bathing suit, and prepare for a truly relaxing experience that blends history, culture, and wellness.

Carrera del Darro

Lined with historic buildings, rustic cafes, and views of the Alhambra, Carrera del Darro is considered Granada's most romantic street. Winding along the Darro River, this cobblestone path is as charming as it is historic. The street dates back to the Arab era and serves as a silent witness to the city's rich past.

As you stroll down Carrera del Darro, make sure to take in the sights of El Bañuelo, the city's best-preserved Arab baths, and the Archaeological Museum housed in a 16th-century palace. The numerous bridges crossing the river, such as the picturesque Puente del Cadí, offer postcard-worthy views of the Alhambra perched on the hillside.

Visiting during early morning or late evening allows you to see the Alhambra bathed in the golden glow of sunrise or sunset, a truly unforgettable sight. Remember to wear comfortable shoes as the cobblestones can be tricky to navigate.

Granada Cuisine

Granada's culinary scene is a delectable blend of cultures, reflecting its Moorish past and Spanish identity. The city is famed for its tapas culture; it's one of the few places in Spain where tapas are served free with every drink order. Each bar tends to have its specialty, offering a chance to embark on a gastronomic journey with each visit.

One of the must-try dishes is 'habas con jamón' (broad beans with ham), a classic Granadian dish symbolizing the blend of Muslim and Christian influences. For those with a sweet tooth, 'Piononos', small cakes named after Pope Pius IX and soaked in syrup and topped with cream, are a local treat originating from the nearby town of Santa Fe.

Beyond the city center, the Albayzín district is perfect for tasting Moroccan influenced cuisine, while the Sacromonte neighborhood is known for its cave restaurants, serving up hearty 'Zambra' style dishes, often accompanied by a flamenco show.

Granada is also known for its locally produced wines, especially from the Contraviesa-Alpujarra region. These high-altitude vineyards produce exceptional vintages that perfectly accompany the local cuisine.

Foodies should consider a guided tapas tour for a curated experience or simply follow their instincts and appetites. Either way, dining in Granada is an adventure of flavors, with each bite capturing a piece of the city's diverse culinary heritage.

Final Thoughts

With its stunning landscapes, rich history, and unique cultural blend, Granada is more than just a travel destination; it's a sensory experience that seizes your heart and soul. This city, where Moorish and Christian cultures have intertwined for centuries, offers a compelling narrative of coexistence and evolution, told through its streets, buildings, and food.

Exploring Granada beyond the main sights yields many rewards. Visit the 'Carmenes' of the Albayzín, traditional Andalusian houses with secret gardens that offer tranquility and a glimpse into local life. For panoramic views of the city, climb up to the San Miguel Alto viewpoint, and watch as the sunset paints the Alhambra in shades of gold.

Attend a 'Zambra' Flamenco show in the Sacromonte caves for an unforgettable night of passion and artistry. Shop for traditional crafts in Alcaicería, the old silk market, where you can find unique souvenirs such as Fajalauza ceramics and Granada-style taracea woodwork.

Don't forget to slow down and simply absorb the city's unique atmosphere. Take time to wander, sip coffee in charming plazas, and engage in 'la sobremesa', the Spanish tradition of relaxing and chatting after a meal. Enjoy the unexpected moments - a sudden view of the Alhambra, the fragrance of jasmine on a quiet street, the sound of a guitar echoing in the evening air. These are the heartbeats of Granada, a city that echoes with the past but pulses vibrantly in the present.

From the majestic Alhambra to the narrow alleyways of Albayzín, from the lively tapas bars to the tranquil tea houses, Granada enchants at every turn. As you prepare to depart, you'll find that a piece of your heart remains, forever entwined with the spirit of this timeless city. In Granada, the tale of two cultures continues, and it's one that you'll be eager to return and read again and again.

CHAPTER 7:
Santiago de Compostela

Nestled in the verdant region of Galicia, in Spain's northwest corner, lies Santiago de Compostela - a city that brims with profound historical, cultural, and spiritual significance. For centuries, it has served as the hallowed conclusion to the legendary Camino de Santiago, a vast network of ancient pilgrimage paths that crisscross Europe, culminating at the city's imposing cathedral. Yet, to understand Santiago de Compostela is to acknowledge that its allure extends far beyond its status as a revered pilgrimage site. This is a city of contrasts, where cobbled, centuries-old passageways harmoniously coexist with a pulsating, contemporary spirit, mirroring its dual identity as both a UNESCO World Heritage site and a bustling university town. Santiago de Compostela's old town, with its stone-clad streets and grand plazas, invites visitors into a captivating chronicle of time. Its architectural tableau is a testament to the city's rich past, displaying a visual symphony of Romanesque, Gothic, and Baroque styles, with the awe-inspiring Santiago Cathedral towering as the city's spiritual and architectural cornerstone. Every corner, every stone of this well-preserved old town whispers tales - tales of weary yet determined pilgrims, tales of scholarly pursuits in venerable institutions, tales of traditional Galician life, and tales of an effervescent modern cultural scene that refuses to be overshadowed by the city's storied past.

Venture beyond its historical heart, and Santiago de Compostela continues to enchant. The city's bustling food markets, like the beloved Mercado de Abastos, are gastronomic playgrounds, teeming with fresh produce from the Galician countryside and the Atlantic Ocean that laps its coasts. Santiago's tapas bars, dotted throughout the city, are social and culinary hubs, where locals and visitors alike congregate over plates of pulpo a feira (octopus) and glasses of Albariño.

For those seeking tranquillity, the city's numerous parks and green spaces offer respite from urban exploration. The Alameda Park, in particular, with its ancient trees and sweeping views of the old town, is a favorite amongst locals for leisurely strolls and quiet contemplation. Additionally, Santiago de Compostela's location provides easy access to the ruggedly beautiful Galician coast, with destinations like the dramatic Cape Finisterre, known as the "End of the World" in Roman times, just a short trip away.

Yet, perhaps the most striking aspect of Santiago de Compostela is its intangible yet palpable essence. It's found in the clinking of the botafumeiro, the cathedral's famous incense burner, in the camaraderie shared over a communal meal in a local tavern, in the quiet, early morning hours as the city still slumbers, and in the jubilant smiles of pilgrims who have completed their arduous journey. This essence, a blend of enduring tradition and dynamic modernity, is the city's true magic.

As we embark on this journey through Santiago de Compostela, we invite you to discover the city that has captured the hearts of pilgrims and travelers for over a thousand years. From its spiritual roots to its vibrant contemporary culture, Santiago de Compostela offers a wealth of unforgettable experiences that reward every journey, whether it's a pilgrimage of faith, a quest for cultural insights, or simply a desire to explore one of Spain's most captivating destinations.

Santiago Cathedral

Nestled within Santiago de Compostela's enchanting old town, the Santiago Cathedral stands as a beacon of the city's profound spiritual significance. The cathedral's imposing edifice, a grand architectural fusion of Romanesque, Gothic, and Baroque styles, provides a visual feast. However, it is within the cathedral's ancient walls that the real magic resides.

Walking into the cathedral is akin to stepping into a world filled with grandeur, history, and a palpable sense of the divine. Visitors are immediately greeted by the Pórtico de la Gloria, the cathedral's famous entryway. The ornately sculpted arch, completed in the 12th century, depicts scenes from the Bible, offering a glimpse into the rich religious narratives of the time.

Beyond the grand entryway, the cathedral's interior continues to mesmerize. The Main Chapel, adorned with a grand altarpiece, is a masterpiece of Spanish Baroque style, while the soaring vaults and intricate stained-glass windows imbue the cathedral with a celestial glow. However, the most sought-after destination for many is the crypt, home to the shrine of St. James, whose remains are believed to rest here, drawing pilgrims from around the world to venerate the apostle.

Don't forget to embrace the tradition of hugging the statue of St. James, located behind the main altar, a symbolic act of gratitude upon completing the pilgrimage. Before you leave, also be sure to witness the spectacle of the botafumeiro, the cathedral's giant incense burner. Swung by eight men, the botafumeiro fills the cathedral with a fragrant haze, a sight that, once witnessed, is not easily forgotten.

The cathedral is an active place of worship, so be sure to respect religious services. Also, note that the botafumeiro is not swung during all services, so check the schedule in advance if you wish to experience this unique event.

The Legendary Camino de Santiago

The Camino de Santiago, or the Way of St. James, is more than just a long-distance trail. It is a journey that transcends geographical and cultural borders, uniting pilgrims from every corner of the globe in a common quest for spiritual enlightenment. For over a thousand years, these paths have served as a conduit, guiding the faithful towards the hallowed grounds of the Santiago Cathedral.

The Camino is not a singular path but rather a web of routes that extend across Europe, all leading to Santiago de Compostela. The most popular of these is the Camino Francés, which stretches some 800 kilometers from Saint-Jean-Pied-de-Port in France to Santiago. Walking this route is a challenging endeavor, with pilgrims traversing diverse landscapes, from the rugged Pyrenees mountains to the vineyards of La Rioja, to the verdant hills of Galicia.

Regardless of the chosen path, the Camino experience is as much about the journey as it is the destination. Along the way, pilgrims encounter historical landmarks, serene countryside, and vibrant cities. Even more importantly, they forge bonds with fellow travelers, sharing stories, meals, and mutual encouragement.

If you plan to walk the Camino, ensure you're adequately prepared. This includes having the right gear, such as comfortable walking shoes, as well as training beforehand. Also, remember to collect stamps on your 'pilgrim's passport' along the way, as you'll need this to receive your Compostela certificate upon reaching Santiago.

City of Culture of Galicia

Stepping into the City of Culture of Galicia, visitors find themselves transported into an awe-inspiring amalgamation of art, technology, and knowledge. Located on Mount Gaiás, this avant-garde architectural complex is a testament to Galicia's investment in preserving its cultural heritage while embracing the future.

Designed by renowned architect Peter Eisenman, the City of Culture is a true architectural marvel. Its design, an intricate maze of winding pathways and undulating roofs, draws inspiration from the medieval streets of Santiago de Compostela. Covering a vast area, the complex houses several key buildings including the Museum of Galicia, the Library of Galicia, and the Galician Archive.

Each visit to the City of Culture offers a unique experience. From exploring Galician history at the museum to admiring panoramic views from the rooftop terraces, there's much to see and do. Art and technology enthusiasts will appreciate the regular exhibitions and workshops that promote innovation and creativity. Wear comfortable shoes as the area is extensive and involves some uphill walking. There is an on-site café where you can take a break and enjoy the impressive views of Santiago.

Mercado de Abastos

After the Santiago Cathedral, the Mercado de Abastos holds the title as the second most visited site in Santiago de Compostela. Bustling with activity, this vibrant market is the heartbeat of the city's culinary scene. Here, locals and visitors alike come to sample and purchase the region's fresh produce.

Housed within a series of granite buildings, the market boasts over 300 stalls selling a variety of goods. From the catch of the day to farm-fresh vegetables, local cheese, and Galician wine, the Mercado de Abastos is a haven for food lovers. The air is filled with the tantalizing aromas of fresh herbs, spices, and baked goods, stimulating the senses.

Perhaps the market's most unique feature is its 'Sea to Market' service. Customers can purchase seafood directly from the coast via video call, and the fresh catch is delivered to the market within hours. For an authentic taste of Galician life, a visit to the Mercado de Abastos is a must. Arrive early in the morning for the best selection. Don't miss the opportunity to try pulpo a la gallega (octopus Galician style), a local delicacy.

Alameda Park

The Alameda Park, located near the old town, is a verdant oasis offering a respite from Santiago's bustling streets. This beautifully manicured park has been a favourite among locals for centuries, serving as a tranquil space for relaxation, recreation, and social gatherings.

As you stroll along its leafy promenades, you'll discover a variety of flora, charming fountains, and sculptures, including the iconic 'Two Marias' statue. From the park, you can also enjoy stunning views of the Santiago Cathedral, particularly from the Paseo de la Herradura, a popular viewpoint.

Whether you're keen on a leisurely walk, a picnic, or simply people-watching, Alameda Park provides the perfect setting. Its tranquillity, combined with its accessibility, make it a cherished part of Santiago's urban landscape. Don't forget to pack a picnic and a book. The park's benches and lawns provide perfect spots for a leisurely lunch and a relaxing afternoon.

Day Trip to Cape Finisterre

Venturing out of Santiago de Compostela for a day trip to Cape Finisterre promises an experience like no other. Hailed as the 'End of the World' by the Romans, this striking cape juts out into the vast Atlantic Ocean, offering a setting of remarkable solitude and profound depth.

The journey to Cape Finisterre navigates through the idyllic Galician countryside, abundant with quaint hamlets and the region's signature undulating landscapes. Upon reaching the cape, one is met with unending views of the expansive ocean, a sight that's particularly spellbinding during sunset.

The lighthouse perched on the cliff adds to the dramatic scenery, standing as a beacon at the edge of the known world. Remember to bring along some warm clothing, as the cape can get windy, regardless of the season. Also, if time permits, pay a visit to the nearby town of Finisterre, known for its seafood cuisine.

The Old Quarter

Immersing oneself in the Old Quarter of Santiago de Compostela is akin to stepping back in time. This historic heart of the city, marked by narrow, winding alleys, atmospheric plazas, and venerable buildings, hums with the echoes of yesteryears.

Recognised as a UNESCO World Heritage Site, the Old Quarter serves as an open-air museum, laying out Santiago's rich cultural and historical narrative. Each square within the quarter emanates a unique allure, inviting exploration and discovery.

Walking is undoubtedly the best way to experience the Old Quarter. Be sure to explore the numerous hidden courtyards, shops selling local crafts, and traditional tapas bars. And don't miss the chance to attend the Pilgrim's Mass at the Cathedral if it coincides with your visit.

The University

The University of Santiago de Compostela, one of the oldest and most prestigious universities in Spain, stands as a monument to the city's long-standing scholarly tradition. Its sprawling campus is an amalgamation of stately historic buildings and modern facilities, reflecting the institute's seamless blend of tradition and innovation.

As you walk through its corridors and courtyards, you are treading the same path as countless scholars and intellectuals who have contributed significantly to various fields over the centuries. The university's library, in particular, is a treasure trove of knowledge, housing an impressive collection of books and manuscripts.

Visitors are welcome to tour the university grounds and buildings. Try to plan your visit during one of the many cultural events or academic conferences that the university hosts. These events often provide intriguing insights into Spain's academic culture and offer a chance to interact with the students and faculty.

The Way of St. James

The Camino de Santiago, or the Way of St. James, is not just a route leading to the Santiago de Compostela Cathedral, it is a transformative journey etched with personal discoveries, camaraderie, and spiritual growth. A tradition stretching back to the Middle Ages, this pilgrimage remains a vital part of the city's identity.

The experience of walking the Camino is as varied as the pilgrims themselves, with paths winding through mountains, plains, and villages, each providing a unique perspective on the Spanish landscape. Completing the pilgrimage, whether for religious, personal, or cultural reasons, often instills a sense of accomplishment and reflection.

For those considering embarking on the Camino, it's important to prepare both physically and mentally. Be sure to pack light, bring comfortable shoes, and have a clear understanding of the route you intend to follow. And remember, the Camino is as much about the journey as it is about the destination.

Hostal dos Reis Católicos

When it comes to unique accommodations, the Hostal dos Reis Católicos takes the crown. Situated in the Praza do Obradoiro, opposite the Santiago de Compostela Cathedral, this five-star hotel holds the distinction of being the oldest hotel in the world. Originally constructed in 1499 as a hospital to tend to the weary pilgrims journeying along the Camino de Santiago, it has now been transformed into a luxurious hotel that still retains its historical charm. The facade of the building is an exquisite example of Plateresque style, and the four courtyards within provide a peaceful retreat.

Staying at the Hostal dos Reis Católicos is like stepping back in time, with each room boasting its own unique features. While booking a room here might be a bit of a splurge, even if you're not staying overnight, consider dining at their restaurant for a taste of Galician cuisine in an atmospheric setting.

Santiago Cuisine

An integral part of Santiago's charm lies in its gastronomy. The city offers a palette of flavors that reflect the region's agricultural wealth and coastal bounty, combined with time-honored culinary traditions. When it comes to food in Santiago, you are in for a feast of Galician cuisine.

Seafood is a standout feature of Galician cuisine, with dishes like Pulpo a la Gallega (octopus with paprika and olive oil), and shellfish prepared in various ways. Meat lovers can delight in the hearty Galician stew (Caldo Gallego) and the famed Ternera Gallega, a top-quality local beef.

Empanadas Gallegas, savory pies with various fillings, are also a popular local staple. For dessert, Santiago is famous for its Tarta de Santiago, an almond cake typically adorned with the cross of Saint James. This sweet treat is the perfect accompaniment to a cup of coffee in one of the city's cozy cafes.

Tapas bars and restaurants are plentiful in the Old Quarter, offering a lively dining scene. Tasting your way through the city is a delightful experience in itself. However, for those interested in a more hands-on approach, consider joining a cooking class or a food tour to delve deeper into the local cuisine.

It is also worth noting that Galicia is a renowned wine-producing region. While in Santiago, don't miss the chance to sample local wines, particularly the Albariño, a white wine known for its aromatic, fresh character. For a more immersive experience, consider visiting one of the many vineyards in the region.

In Santiago, every meal has the potential to turn into a culinary journey, celebrating the region's abundant produce and the Galicians' passion for food. Whether it's enjoying tapas with new-found friends or savoring a leisurely meal in a fine dining restaurant, Santiago's gastronomy is sure to leave a lasting impression.

Final Thoughts

In Santiago de Compostela, every stone tells a story, every street leads to a discovery, and every journey, regardless of its starting point, seems to find its conclusion. This ancient city, nestled in the green heart of Galicia, is a symbol of perseverance, spirituality, and the constant dialogue between the past and the present.

Wandering the streets of Santiago's old town is like stepping back in time. Its centuries-old buildings, each more captivating than the last, coexist harmoniously with lively bars, boutique shops, and modern cultural institutions. Every corner of this UNESCO World Heritage site offers an opportunity to delve deeper into the rich tapestry of Galician history and culture.

Beyond the city's historical and religious landmarks, Santiago de Compostela also offers a range of modern amenities and experiences. The Auditorio de Galicia, located in the Vista Alegre Park, regularly hosts concerts and other cultural events. For shopping enthusiasts, the area around the Rua do Franco offers a blend of local and international shops, along with several unique Galician crafts boutiques.

For nature enthusiasts, Santiago's numerous parks and green spaces provide a welcome respite from the hustle and bustle of city life. The Park of San Domingos de Bonaval, located on a hillside, offers great views over the city and houses the Museum of the Galician People. Similarly, a walk along the Sar River offers a quieter, more natural perspective of Santiago.

Whether you're here to embark on the spiritual journey of the Camino de Santiago, explore the depth of Galician culture, or simply enjoy the city's unique blend of history and modernity, Santiago de Compostela offers an experience like no other. Its compelling blend of the sacred and the secular, the ancient and the contemporary, the cultural and the natural, ensures that there is something for every traveler.

To truly capture the essence of Santiago, take the time to sit in one of its plazas, sip on a glass of Albariño, and watch as pilgrims of all walks of life conclude their journey. This simple yet profound experience encapsulates what Santiago de Compostela is all about: a city where journeys end, memories begin, and the spirit of the Camino lives on.

CHAPTER 8:
San Sebastián

San Sebastián, or Donostia as it's known in the Basque language, is the embodiment of sophistication and charm. Nestled on the northern coast of Spain, this elegant seaside city harmoniously combines natural beauty with cultural dynamism, making it a captivating destination for travelers worldwide. With its stunning Belle Époque architecture, pristine sandy beaches, and world-class culinary scene, San Sebastián is undoubtedly the pearl of the Basque Country.

One of the city's most captivating features is its stunning natural setting. Framed by the crystal-clear waters of the Bay of Biscay and encircled by lush, rolling hills, San Sebastián's scenery is a feast for the eyes. The city is perfectly situated for exploring the broader Basque region, with its dramatic landscapes, ancient traditions, and unique language.

At the heart of San Sebastián lies its Old Town, or Parte Vieja, a bustling hub teeming with narrow alleys, centuries-old buildings, and a plethora of pintxos bars serving up the region's delicious cuisine. Here, history reverberates through the walls, from the imposing Baroque facade of the Basilica of Saint Mary of the Chorus to the quaint charm of Constitution Square.

Yet, San Sebastián is not a city that rests on its historical laurels. It has also positioned itself as a modern cultural capital. Whether you're exploring the cutting-edge exhibitions at

Tabakalera Contemporary Culture Centre, catching a film at the prestigious San Sebastián International Film Festival, or simply strolling through the vibrant streets soaking in the atmosphere, the city pulsates with cultural energy.

Despite all its natural and cultural wealth, what truly sets San Sebastián apart is its status as a gastronomic powerhouse. With more Michelin stars per capita than almost anywhere else in the world, it's a veritable paradise for food lovers. But whether you're dining in a high-end restaurant or enjoying pintxos at a local bar, the emphasis is always on quality, local produce, and the celebration of Basque culinary traditions.

In summary, San Sebastián is a city that effortlessly captures the imagination. Its blend of natural beauty, historic charm, cultural vitality, and culinary prowess makes it a must-visit destination. Whether you're a nature lover, history buff, culture vulture, or foodie, San Sebastián has something special to offer you. Now, let's delve deeper into what makes this Basque gem truly shine.

La Concha Beach

Often cited as one of the world's most beautiful urban beaches, La Concha Beach is an iconic part of San Sebastián. Its name, meaning "The Shell" in Spanish, perfectly describes its crescent-shaped coastline, framing the azure waters of the Bay of Biscay. Lined with white sand and punctuated by the scenic Santa Clara Island in the bay's center, the beach offers postcard-worthy views at every turn.

La Concha is perfect for a range of beach activities, from sunbathing and swimming to paddleboarding and kayaking. The beach is known for its calm, clear waters, thanks to the protective presence of the Santa Clara Island and the two montes—

Monte Igueldo and Monte Urgull—that flank it. The picturesque promenade running alongside the beach is perfect for leisurely strolls, with several cafes and ice cream parlors en route. When planning your visit to La Concha Beach, keep in mind that it can get quite crowded during the summer months, especially in August. Arriving early in the day can help you secure a good spot. Also, don't forget to explore the charming gardens of Miramar Palace located nearby, offering an elevated view of the beach.

Old Town

San Sebastián's Old Town, or Parte Vieja, is a maze of narrow, winding streets, packed with historic buildings, vibrant pintxos bars, and specialty shops. This compact neighborhood is the city's beating heart, where the past meets the present in a dynamic fusion of history, culture, and gastronomy.

The Old Town is home to some of the city's most iconic landmarks, including the robust San Vicente Church, considered the oldest in the city, and the Constitution Square, previously a bullfighting arena. The square's balconies still bear numbers from the time when spectators would rent them for viewing the bullfights.

Exploring the Old Town is best done on foot, meandering through its pedestrian-friendly streets and taking in the atmosphere. Be sure to try the renowned pintxos—small snacks traditionally skewered to a slice of bread—in the many bars that line the streets. For a different perspective of the area, consider joining a guided tour, which will offer insights into the rich history and culinary traditions of the Old Town.

Monte Igueldo

Monte Igueldo offers the most breathtaking panoramic views of San Sebastián. Rising majestically at the western end of La Concha Bay, this hill serves as a fantastic viewpoint, overlooking the city's charming urban layout, the sparkling bay, and the surrounding verdant hills.

At the top of Monte Igueldo, you'll find an old-fashioned amusement park with vintage rides and attractions that have been enchanting visitors for over a century. However, the real draw is the hill's vantage point, from where you can capture spectacular photos, especially at sunrise or sunset.

To reach the top of Monte Igueldo, you can take the charming old funicular railway, which has been in operation since 1912. The journey itself is a delightful experience, offering increasingly impressive views as you ascend. Remember to pack a picnic to enjoy at the summit, and, of course, don't forget your camera to capture the unforgettable vistas.

San Sebastián International Film Festival

Every September, San Sebastián transforms into a bustling film capital as it hosts the prestigious San Sebastián International Film Festival. Established in 1953, this event is one of the most important film festivals in the world, alongside Cannes, Venice, and Berlin, and has become a significant platform for showcasing Basque, Spanish, and Latin American films.

The festival brings together a constellation of stars and industry professionals who gather for the celebration of cinema. From premieres and screenings to workshops and parties, the festival is a vibrant affair, illuminating the city with its glitz and glamour.

If you're planning to attend the San Sebastián International Film Festival, it's recommended to book your tickets and accommodations in advance as the city becomes particularly busy during this period. Additionally, take the opportunity to explore the iconic venues of the festival, such as the Kursaal Congress Centre and Auditorium and the Victoria Eugenia Theatre, both architectural masterpieces in their own right.

San Telmo Museum

The San Telmo Museum serves as a treasure trove of Basque culture and history. Housed in a 16th-century Dominican convent, with a modern extension that seamlessly merges the old with the new, this museum provides a comprehensive overview of the Basque Country's rich heritage.

Inside, you'll find a vast collection that spans prehistory to the present, featuring artifacts, artworks, and multimedia displays. The museum's exhibitions offer fascinating insights into the Basque people's traditions, language, and way of life, as well as the region's natural history.

When visiting the San Telmo Museum, take your time to explore the exhibitions thoroughly. The museum offers audio guides and has plenty of explanatory panels, most of which are translated into English. Also, don't miss the chance to appreciate the building itself, especially the contemporary wing designed by the architects Nieto Sobejano, which is a masterpiece of modern architecture.

Day Trip to Pasaia

A short drive or a scenic boat ride east of San Sebastián will take you to Pasaia, a charming coastal town steeped in maritime tradition. Nestled in a narrow fjord-like bay, Pasaia is composed of four districts, each with its unique character. Donibane and San Pedro, located on opposite sides of the bay, are particularly worth visiting.

The town is known for its well-preserved historic architecture, vibrant fishing port, and the Albaola Sea Factory, where visitors can watch the construction of historical ships using traditional methods. Literary enthusiasts will also enjoy visiting the house-museum of the French author Victor Hugo, who was enchanted by Pasaia during his visit in 1843.

A day trip to Pasaia offers a wonderful opportunity to immerse yourself in authentic Basque maritime culture. Remember to try the town's excellent seafood, particularly the txipirones (squid) and bacalao a la pasaitarra (cod in a local sauce). For an unforgettable experience, consider the boat ride back to San Sebastián at sunset when the views of the coastline are especially enchanting.

La Bretxa Market

The vibrant La Bretxa Market offers a tantalizing window into the culinary world of San Sebastián and the Basque Country. Located in the Old Town, the market is housed in a historic building that combines 19th-century architecture with modern additions.

Stroll through the bustling aisles and you'll encounter a plethora of fresh, locally-sourced produce: from colourful vegetables and ripe fruits to a range of meats and the freshest seafood. You can also find artisan cheeses, olives, spices, and a range of local delicacies. Upstairs, there are shops selling clothes and household goods.

Visiting La Bretxa Market is an experience, and taking the time to explore its offerings will provide you with a vivid understanding of Basque gastronomy. To get the best produce, try to arrive in the morning when the market is busiest. And don't forget to pick up some local delicacies to enjoy later or as unique edible souvenirs from your visit.

Peine del Viento

The Peine del Viento, or the Wind Comb, is one of San Sebastián's most iconic landmarks. Located at the foot of Monte Igueldo, this remarkable sculpture is the work of Basque artist Eduardo Chillida and architect Luis Peña Ganchegui. It comprises three iron sculptures, firmly anchored to the rocks, braving the relentless waves and wind.

The artistic creation, with its dramatic play of nature and art, embodies the spirit of the Basque Country. The sculptures also serve as vents for an underground network of tunnels, which, when hit by the waves, create a unique symphony of sounds and a spectacle of water sprays.

Visiting the Peine del Viento at different times of day offers varying experiences; however, the dramatic view of the sculpture against the sunset is particularly memorable. There are also several cafes and restaurants nearby where you can enjoy a meal or a coffee while admiring the scenic views.

Miramar Palace

Perched atop a hill overlooking La Concha Bay, Miramar Palace is a symbol of the city's history and grandeur. The palace was designed in the late 19th century by the English architect Selden Wornum for the Spanish royal family, reflecting an English country house style that stands out among the predominantly Basque architecture of the city.

Surrounded by lush gardens, the palace offers breathtaking views of the city and the bay. Today, the building is owned by the city council and used for various cultural events, while the gardens are open to the public.

During your visit to the Miramar Palace, make sure to stroll around the beautiful gardens and enjoy the panoramic views. The palace is also located near the start of the scenic walk to the Peine del Viento, so consider combining the two visits. Also, the palace is most easily accessible by foot or bike, as parking can be challenging in the area.

Tabakalera

Situated in a restored former tobacco factory, Tabakalera is a hub for contemporary culture in San Sebastián. Today, this vast space is devoted to creation, training, and research into contemporary art across multiple disciplines - from visual arts and film to dance and performance arts.

The Tabakalera is more than just an art centre; it's a dynamic space that invites the public to interact with art and artists. It features exhibition halls, workshops, performance spaces, and a cinema specializing in independent films. There's also a library, a restaurant, and a café within the premises.

When you visit Tabakalera, take time to explore the rotating exhibitions, attend a performance or film screening, or even participate in a workshop. Check their website in advance to see what's on. And don't forget to visit the rooftop terrace, which offers panoramic views over San Sebastián.

San Sebastián Cuisine

Food in San Sebastián is not just a matter of sustenance, but a way of life. The city is renowned worldwide for its gastronomy, boasting more Michelin stars per square metre than any other city, save Kyoto, Japan. But the culinary culture here extends well beyond the upscale dining rooms of Michelin-starred restaurants.

The city's Old Town, known as Parte Vieja, is brimming with pintxos bars, serving up the Basque version of tapas. These bite-sized delights range from traditional offerings like anchovies and olives to miniature culinary masterpieces that showcase the creativity of local chefs. Pintxos bar hopping is a beloved local tradition and an experience not to be missed.

Seafood is a pillar of San Sebastián's cuisine, thanks to the city's coastal location. Local favourites include hake cheek, baby squid, and cod, typically cooked simply to let the quality of the ingredients shine through. Don't miss out on trying the famous Basque cheesecake, a creamy and caramelized delight that has gained global fame.

Another essential food experience in San Sebastián is dining at a txoko, or gastronomic society. These private clubs are places where members come together to cook, eat, and socialize. Some txokos open their doors to tourists for a truly local dining experience.

A visit to San Sebastián would not be complete without exploring the city's food markets. Here, you'll find the fresh, high-quality ingredients that form the basis of Basque cuisine. La Bretxa and San Martín markets are two of the most popular, offering a range of local produce, meat, and seafood.

In San Sebastián, food is a celebration of the city's culture, heritage, and the bounty of its surrounding land and sea. Whether you're savoring a pintxo at a bustling bar, indulging in a Michelin-starred meal, or picking up fresh produce at a market, you're participating in a culinary tradition that's at the heart of life in this Basque city.

Final Thoughts

As your journey through San Sebastián comes to a close, you'll likely find yourself captivated by the city's charming mix of natural beauty, cultural richness, and unparalleled gastronomic scene. The city's inherent sophistication extends beyond its refined architecture and high-end dining; it can be found in the rhythm of life along its sandy beaches, in its buzzing pintxos bars, and even in the quiet elegance of its tree-lined streets.

There is much more to explore in San Sebastián than could be encapsulated in this guide. From the aquarium that offers a glimpse into the marine life of the Bay of Biscay, to the numerous festivals like Jazzaldia, the city's international jazz festival, and Semana Grande, a week-long celebration filled with music, fireworks and traditional Basque sports.

Active travellers might enjoy surfing at Zurriola Beach, known for its excellent waves, or kayaking in the Bay of La Concha. Alternatively, consider cycling along the network of bike lanes that crisscross the city, offering an eco-friendly way to explore at your own pace.

When in San Sebastián, be sure to take the time to simply stroll along its streets, take in the architecture, and immerse yourself in its atmosphere. The charm of San Sebastián is as much in its everyday moments as it is in its landmarks. Visit the local markets, stop for a café con leche in a sun-drenched plaza, or simply watch the world go by from a bench on the promenade.

While this guide provides an overview of what San Sebastián has to offer, the true magic of the city lies in the unique experiences you'll stumble upon during your visit. So embrace the Basque way of life, indulge in the gastronomic delights, and let the spirit of San Sebastián captivate you.

San Sebastián is not just a destination, but a feeling – one that's sure to leave a lasting impression long after you've returned home. So here's to the memories you're about to create and the enchanting allure of San Sebastián – the sophisticated seaside city that's waiting to welcome you.

SPAIN TRAVEL GUIDE

CHAPTER 9:
Córdoba

• • • • • • • • • • • • • •

Lying in the heart of Andalusia, Córdoba is a city that has seen the rise and fall of empires. A UNESCO World Heritage city, Córdoba is a captivating blend of cultures, a testament to its rich history as a centre of Roman, Moorish, and Christian civilizations. As you walk its narrow, winding streets, you'll feel the echoes of its past, reflected in the harmony of its architectural treasures and the spirit of its people.

Once the capital of the Islamic Emirate and then Caliphate in the Iberian Peninsula, Córdoba was a beacon of learning and culture, boasting an unprecedented mix of libraries, universities, and medical schools. This intellectual fervour has left its mark on the city, which, today, is an inspiring blend of the past and the present.

At the heart of Córdoba lies the Mezquita, an architectural marvel that encapsulates the city's cultural syncretism. Once a mosque, now a cathedral, the Mezquita is a tangible embodiment of Córdoba's layered history. But this is just one of many gems you'll find in Córdoba; the city is replete with historic landmarks, from the royal fortress of Alcázar de los Reyes Cristianos to the ruins of the Umayyad city of Medina Azahara.

Yet Córdoba is more than its monuments. It is a living city, pulsating with energy and colour. Each May, the city erupts in a riot of colours during the Festival de los Patios, when residents open their private courtyards, adorned with vibrant flowers, to the public. These courtyards, or patios, are another symbol of Córdoba's distinct culture, offering a unique blend of Arabic and Andalusian traditions.

Córdoba's charm extends beyond the city itself. Just a short trip away lies the Sierra de Hornachuelos, a natural park that offers a refreshing escape from the urban landscape. Here, you can explore lush Mediterranean forests, spot local wildlife, and even visit some of the charming rural villages nestled within the park.

A visit to Córdoba is a journey through history, a chance to experience the melting pot of cultures that have shaped its identity. Whether you're exploring its ancient landmarks, wandering through its picturesque patios, or indulging in the local cuisine, Córdoba promises an unforgettable journey into the heart of Andalusian culture.

The Mezquita

Stepping into the Mezquita of Córdoba is like traversing the history of Andalusian architecture in a single visit. Originally built as a Visigothic church in the 6th century, it was converted into a mosque following the Islamic conquest, and then transformed again into a Catholic cathedral in the 13th century. Its architectural style reflects this historical timeline, resulting in a unique fusion of Gothic, Islamic, and Renaissance elements.

The heart of the Mezquita is its expansive prayer hall, filled with a forest of red and white arches that create an optical illusion of infinite space. The mihrab, or prayer niche, is an intricately decorated masterpiece of Islamic art, contrasted by the towering Renaissance altarpiece that now dominates the centre of the building. Walking through this architectural marvel, one can't help but feel a sense of awe at the interplay of cultures.

To get the most out of your visit to the Mezquita, consider hiring a guide or downloading an audio guide, which can provide in-depth information about its history and architecture. The site can get crowded, especially during the peak tourist season, so aim for an early morning or late afternoon visit. Don't forget to take a moment to sit and absorb the unique atmosphere of this remarkable place.

Alcázar de los Reyes Cristianos

Córdoba's Alcázar de los Reyes Cristianos, or Castle of the Christian Monarchs, is a regal edifice that bears witness to some of the most pivotal moments in Spain's history. Built in the 14th century by Alfonso XI, it served as the primary residence of Ferdinand and Isabella, and it was here that they met with Christopher Columbus before his famous voyage to the New World. The Alcázar's austere military exterior belies the beauty that awaits within. Its stunning gardens, filled with ponds, fountains, and lush vegetation, provide a tranquil retreat from the city's hustle and bustle. The fortress itself houses a collection of Roman mosaics and sarcophagi, as well as the haunting Royal Baths, illuminated by star-shaped skylights.

When visiting the Alcázar, be sure to climb to the top of the towers for a panoramic view of Córdoba, with the Mezquita and the Guadalquivir River creating a picture-perfect backdrop. Try to time your visit to enjoy the gardens at sunset when they take on a magical glow.

Medina Azahara

Located on the outskirts of Córdoba, the ruins of Medina Aza-hara offer a glimpse into the opulence of the Umayyad Caliph-ate. Built in the 10th century by Caliph Abd ar-Rahman III, this once-magnificent city was a symbol of power and wealth, with its name meaning "The Shining City."

Today, the remains of the palaces, mosques, and administrative buildings are a poignant reminder of the city's former grandeur. Despite the ravages of time, you can still marvel at the detailed carvings, ornate arches, and intricate tilework that adorn the surviving structures. The site's museum provides valuable con-text and houses artifacts recovered during excavations.

A visit to Medina Azahara requires some planning. It's located about 8 km outside of Córdoba, and public transportation options are limited. It's best to visit with a tour or by car. The site is vast, so wear comfortable shoes, bring plenty of water, and allow enough time to explore. The panoramic views of Córdoba from the site are well worth the trip.

The Roman Bridge

Spanning the Guadalquivir River, the Roman Bridge of Cór-doba is one of the city's most iconic landmarks. Originally con-structed in the 1st century BC, it has been rebuilt and refur-bished multiple times over the centuries, but it still retains its Roman foundation and historical charm. The 16 arches that support the bridge offer an impressive vista and have become a symbol of the city.

Strolling across the Roman Bridge is like taking a walk through time. You'll be treading the same path that Roman soldiers,

Moorish caliphs, and Christian monarchs once used. At the southern end of the bridge, you'll find the Calahorra Tower, a fortified gate that now houses a museum dedicated to Andalusian history.

The bridge offers stunning views of the Mezquita and the Alcázar, particularly during sunrise or sunset. Consider walking the bridge at different times of the day to experience the changing light and atmosphere. The bridge is pedestrianized, so take your time, soak in the sights, and perhaps pause for a photo or two.

The Courtyards

Córdoba's courtyards, or "patios," are an integral part of the city's cultural identity and a delightful spectacle for visitors. These private spaces are lovingly adorned with a profusion of colourful flowers and plants, creating a cool and fragrant haven amidst the city's narrow streets and whitewashed houses. The tradition of decorating patios dates back to Roman and Moorish times and is a unique aspect of Cordoban life.

The courtyards are particularly enchanting during the annual Festival de los Patios, held in May, when residents compete for the title of the most beautiful patio. During this time, many private homes open their doors to allow the public to admire their stunning floral displays.

If you're visiting outside of the festival period, several patios are open year-round. The Palacio de Viana, for example, boasts 12 magnificent courtyards. Do remember to respect the privacy of residents if you're peeking into private patios. It's also worth noting that the vibrancy and variety of the flowers can depend on the time of year.

Day Trip to the Sierra de Hornachuelos

For those craving a break from the city's architectural wonders, a day trip to the Sierra de Hornachuelos Natural Park provides a refreshing change of scenery. Located around an hour's drive from Córdoba, this expansive park is one of the largest protected areas in Andalusia, with landscapes ranging from lush forests and tranquil lakes to rugged cliffs and rolling meadows. The park is home to an impressive array of wildlife, including deer, wild boars, and a variety of bird species, making it a haven for nature lovers. There are numerous trails to explore, catering to hikers of all levels, as well as picnic spots and recreational areas for those who prefer a more leisurely pace.

To reach the Sierra de Hornachuelos, you'll need to rent a car or join a tour, as public transport options are limited. Make sure to pack water, snacks, and a map of the park, as some areas can be quite remote. And, of course, don't forget your camera to capture the park's serene beauty.

The Jewish Quarter

The Jewish Quarter, or "Judería," is one of Córdoba's most fascinating districts. This labyrinth of narrow, winding streets and flower-filled courtyards is steeped in history and offers an intimate glimpse into Córdoba's multicultural past. The quarter dates back to the Middle Ages when it was the center of Jewish life in the city.

Key points of interest within the Jewish Quarter include the ancient Synagogue, one of the few surviving examples in Spain, and the Sephardic House, a museum dedicated to preserving the legacy of the Sephardic Jews. Strolling around, you'll also find delightful artisan shops, traditional taverns, and small plazas.

While exploring, keep an eye out for the statue of Maimonides, a revered Jewish philosopher born in Córdoba. His teachings continue to inspire scholars worldwide. The Jewish Quarter is best explored on foot, allowing you to fully appreciate its unique atmosphere. It's easy to get lost, but that's part of the charm—every corner reveals a new surprise.

Córdoba Synagogue

Córdoba's Synagogue, located in the heart of the Jewish Quarter, stands as a poignant reminder of the city's Sephardic heritage. Built in 1315, it's one of only three medieval synagogues remaining in Spain. While it's small in size, the building's historical and cultural significance is vast.

Inside, visitors can admire the intricate Mudejar plasterwork that adorns its walls, inscribed with Hebrew psalms and floral motifs. Although no longer used for worship, the synagogue's aura of tranquility and reflection remains palpable.

Visiting the synagogue is a sobering experience, providing a deeper understanding of Córdoba's multicultural history. It's a popular tourist attraction, so try to visit early in the day to avoid the largest crowds. Please remember to respect the sanctity of the space during your visit.

Calahorra Tower

Standing guard at the southern end of the Roman Bridge, the Calahorra Tower is one of Córdoba's most distinctive landmarks. Built by the Moors and later reinforced by Christian monarchs, it has served as a defensive structure, a prison, and even a girls' school throughout its long history.

Today, the Calahorra Tower houses the Museum of Al-Andalus Life, which showcases the rich cultural heritage of the region during the period of Muslim rule. Its exhibits cover a range of topics, from science and philosophy to art and daily life, offering a comprehensive insight into this influential era.

The tower's rooftop offers unparalleled views of the Roman Bridge and the Mezquita, making it a must-visit spot for photography enthusiasts. Consider timing your visit for sunset when the view is at its most magical. Be aware that there are many steps to reach the top, but the panoramic vistas are well worth the effort.

The Flower Street

Calleja de las Flores, or the Flower Street, is one of Córdoba's most picturesque spots. Tucked away in the historic center, this narrow, cobblestone alley is a feast for the eyes with its white-washed walls adorned with vibrant flowers in blue pots, echoing Andalusian tradition.

The end of the alley opens up to a small square with a fountain, from where you get a stunning view of the Mezquita's bell tower framed by a cascade of colorful blooms. The sight is particularly beautiful in spring, when the flowers are in full bloom.

Visit early in the morning or late afternoon to avoid the crowds and capture the best photographs. Also, don't forget to explore the surrounding area, which is full of charming shops, cafes, and other hidden alleys just waiting to be discovered.

Córdoba Cuisine

Córdoba's cuisine is a rich tapestry that mirrors its multicultural heritage. With influences from Roman, Arab, and Christian traditions, the local fare offers a gastronomic journey through time. Whether it's the traditional taverns, contemporary eateries, or bustling food markets, the city is a food lover's paradise, offering something to satisfy every palate.

Start with "salmorejo", a thicker, more robust cousin of gazpacho. This creamy, chilled tomato soup, topped with diced Spanish ham and hard-boiled eggs, is a classic Córdoba dish and the perfect antidote to the city's summer heat. Another quintessential local dish is "flamenquín", deep-fried pork or ham rolls that are a staple in the local tapas scene.

For the main course, indulge in "rabobull", a slow-cooked oxtail stew that's deeply comforting and incredibly flavorful. Alternatively, sample the "berenjenas con miel", or aubergines with honey, a delightful balance of savory and sweet that is sure to surprise your palate. Vegetarian and vegan visitors will also find plenty to enjoy, as many restaurants now offer plant-based versions of traditional dishes.

Sweet lovers, be prepared for a treat. Córdoba's dessert offerings, largely influenced by the city's Sephardic Jewish history, are exceptional. The "pastel cordobés", a puff pastry filled with sweet pumpkin jam, is a must-try. Other popular choices include "alfajores", a honey and almond sweet, and "pestiños", deep-fried pastries soaked in honey.

And then, of course, there is the region's excellent wine. Córdoba is part of the Montilla-Moriles denomination, known for its production of "fino", a dry, crisp white wine perfect for pairing with tapas. There are many bodegas (wine bars) where you can sample the local wines and sherries.

Eating in Córdoba is not just about the food, it's a cultural experience. It's about the joy of sharing a meal, the art of conversation, and the tradition of hospitality that is inherent in the Cordobese way of life. So take your time, savour each bite, and let the flavours of Córdoba take you on a journey of discovery.

Final Thoughts

As your journey through Córdoba comes to an end, you'll carry with you memories of a city that has seamlessly blended its Roman, Moorish, and Christian roots into a vibrant and harmonious present. Its cultural richness, architectural splendor, and culinary delights leave a lasting impression on all who visit. While the grandeur of the Mezquita, the beauty of the Alcázar, and the charm of the Flower Street represent the city's historical face, Córdoba also offers a modern, vibrant side. For a change of pace, explore the contemporary district around Tendillas Square, where you can shop for the latest Spanish fashions or enjoy a meal at a trendy rooftop restaurant with stunning views over the city.

Don't forget to visit the traditional craft workshops dotted around the city. These artisanal havens offer a range of beautiful, locally made products from ceramics and textiles to silverware and leather goods. These items make for perfect souvenirs, encapsulating the spirit and craftsmanship of Córdoba.

If you're visiting in May, do try to catch the Festival of the Patios. This unique cultural event, which sees the city's private courtyards turned into public art spaces, beautifully encapsulates the spirit of Córdoba. These floral displays, full of colour and aroma, are a delight for the senses and a testament to the city's enduring love for beauty.

Moreover, the city's position in the heart of Andalusia makes it an excellent base for exploring the region's natural beauty. From Córdoba, it's easy to take day trips to the Sierra de Hornachuelos Natural Park, the vineyards of Montilla-Moriles, or the historical towns of Écija and Priego de Córdoba.

Lastly, remember to embrace the laid-back rhythm of Córdoba. This is a city that invites you to wander through its cobbled streets, pause to listen to the strains of a flamenco guitar, and to enjoy a leisurely meal in a sun-dappled courtyard. Córdoba isn't just a city to be seen, but to be experienced. Take the time to breathe in its history, savour its flavours, and soak in its vibrant culture.

CHAPTER 10:
Spanish Cuisine

To understand Spain is to understand its food. Every bite into the country's rich and diverse culinary offerings is a glimpse into its history, culture, and spirit. From the sizzling paellas of Valencia to the hearty cocidos of Madrid, from the smoky paprika-laced chorizo of Extremadura to the fresh seafood of Galicia, Spanish cuisine is as diverse as the country's landscapes. Each region, with its unique geography and history, has contributed distinct flavours to the national palate. The lush green hills of the north have given us hearty stews and superb cheeses, while the sun-bathed southern regions are famed for their gazpachos and fried fish. The central plains, with their rich soils, provide grains, vegetables, and pulses, forming the backbone of many Spanish dishes.

Yet, there are common threads that bind these culinary traditions together. The love for fresh, locally-sourced ingredients, the mastery over simple yet bold flavours, the joy of communal eating, and an unwavering commitment to preserving age-old cooking traditions. These are the hallmarks of Spanish cuisine.

Spain's relationship with food goes beyond the kitchen. It's woven into the fabric of daily life. It's seen in the lively chatter around tapas bars, the quiet satisfaction of a well-made home-cooked meal, the yearly festivities revolving around food harvests, and the cherished tradition of the mid-afternoon siesta following a hearty lunch.

But Spanish cuisine is not stuck in the past. It is constantly evolving, with a new generation of chefs reimagining traditional dishes in exciting ways and integrating international flavours into their repertoire. This duality of the old and the new, the traditional and the innovative, adds another layer of complexity to the Spanish culinary scene.

Embarking on a culinary journey through Spain is a gastronomic adventure like no other. It's not just about discovering new flavours and dishes, but also about understanding a way of life. So sit back, tuck in your napkin, and prepare to savor the flavourful diversity of Spanish cuisine.

The Tapas Culture

Tapas, the small plates of food accompanied by a drink, are an integral part of Spanish culture. This tradition began in the Andalusian taverns as a simple slice of bread or meat placed over the glass to keep the flies out, hence the name 'tapa', which means lid. Over time, these edible covers evolved into a culinary tradition in their own right, showcasing a vast array of Spanish flavours.

Today, tapas are served in bars and restaurants throughout the country, and each region has its specialities. From olives, almonds, and chorizo in the south, to seafood, cheeses, and pinchos in the north, the variety of tapas is mind-boggling. They are not just food, but a social activity, a reason to get together and share moments.

For a genuine tapas experience, head to a local "tapería" or "cervecería" in any Spanish city or town. Many locals suggest "tapeo" or a "tapas crawl" - moving from bar to bar, trying out different tapas at each stop. Remember, the essence of tapas is not just about what you eat, but also about the lively company and conversation that comes with it.

Seafood

Given its extensive coastline and history of maritime exploration, it's no surprise that seafood holds a significant place in Spanish cuisine. From the cold Atlantic waters to the warmer Mediterranean Sea, each region contributes a variety of seafood to the Spanish table. Mussels, shrimp, octopus, sardines, and the prized bluefin tuna are just a few examples of the country's seafood bounty.

Paella, the famous rice dish from Valencia, often features a mix of seafood, such as prawns, mussels, and squid. In Galicia, a region known for its exceptional seafood, dishes like "pulpo a la gallega" (octopus with paprika) and "empanada de mariscos" (seafood pie) are popular.

For the freshest seafood experience, visit the coastal towns and cities where you can often eat seafood caught on the same day. You can also check out the seafood markets in major cities. For instance, Madrid's Mercado de Maravillas has a stunning range of seafood, despite the city's inland location. In Barcelona, the famous La Boqueria market offers a vibrant seafood selection amidst its bustling stalls.

Olive Oil

Olive oil is more than just a cooking ingredient in Spain—it's a way of life. Spain is the world's largest producer of olive oil, and the golden liquid is a staple in Spanish kitchens, used in everything from frying and baking to salad dressings and even desserts.

The country boasts several olive oil-producing regions, with Andalusia being the largest. Its Jaén province alone produces more olive oil than any other region in the world. Other notable areas include Catalonia, known for its Arbequina olives, and Extremadura, famed for its robust, peppery oils.

For olive oil enthusiasts, a visit to an olive oil mill or "almazara" offers a fascinating glimpse into the production process. Many mills also offer tastings, where you can learn to appreciate the various flavours and aromas of different oils. You can find these mills scattered across the olive-growing regions. Many Spanish supermarkets also have an impressive selection of local olive oils. Remember, when buying olive oil, look for "virgen extra" on the label, the highest quality category.

Traditional Dishes

Spanish cuisine is as diverse as its landscapes, and each region boasts its unique dishes steeped in tradition. In Valencia, Paella, a saffron-infused rice dish usually cooked with rabbit, chicken, and green beans, is a must-try. Equally famous is Andalusia's Gazpacho, a cold tomato-based soup perfect for hot summer days.

In the landlocked region of Castilla y León, you'll find Cocido Maragato, a hearty meat and chickpea stew, turned upside down, with meat served first. Madrid's winter staple, Cocido Madrileño, is another comforting chickpea-based stew with vegetables, meats, and sausages. Further north, in the Basque Country, the traditional dish is Bacalao a la Vizcaína, salt cod in a red pepper sauce.

One way to explore Spain's diverse food culture is to try these regional dishes in their places of origin. However, if traveling is not an option, many local restaurants throughout the country offer regional specialties. Furthermore, cooking classes are an enjoyable way to learn about these traditional dishes. Many cities offer culinary workshops where you can learn the secrets of Spanish cuisine and bring home a piece of this rich culinary tradition.

Spanish Wines

Spain is one of the world's leading wine producers, renowned for its diversity of wine styles and grape varieties. From the full-bodied reds of Rioja to the unique fortified wines of Jerez, Spanish wines offer something for every palate.

Rioja, Spain's most recognized wine region, produces excellent Tempranillo-based red wines known for their ageing potential. In contrast, Jerez de la Frontera in Andalusia is famous for Sherry, a unique fortified wine with styles ranging from the bone-dry Fino to the sweet Pedro Ximénez.

Whether you are a casual wine drinker or a serious oenophile, visiting a local "bodega" or wine cellar can be a memorable experience. Many wineries offer guided tours and tastings, giving visitors the opportunity to learn about the wine-making process and taste the finished product. Alternatively, wine shops and bars in most cities have a broad selection of Spanish wines. Don't hesitate to ask for recommendations—the Spanish are passionate about their wines and often happy to share their knowledge.

Spanish Cheeses

Cheese in Spain is deeply regional, with each area producing its own distinct varieties. Manchego, the most famous Spanish cheese, is a sheep's milk cheese from La Mancha. It's known for its firm texture and a flavor that ranges from mild to sharp depending on its ageing.

Other notable Spanish cheeses include Cabrales, a blue cheese from Asturias aged in natural caves, and Mahón, a cow's milk cheese from Menorca that can be enjoyed young or aged. In the Basque Country and Navarre, the slightly smoked Idiazábal made from sheep's milk is a traditional favourite.

Cheese shops and local markets are the best places to explore the diversity of Spanish cheeses. These venues often provide tastings, allowing you to discover your favourite. Also, consider visiting a local cheese festival, like the National Cheese Festival in Trujillo, Extremadura, where you can try a wide array of Spanish cheeses in one place. Lastly, when enjoying Spanish cheese, remember it pairs excellently with Spanish wines, creating a perfect gastronomic union.

Spanish Desserts

Spanish cuisine is known not only for its savory dishes but also for its delightful desserts. The national favorite is arguably Churros con Chocolate, a fried dough pastry served with a thick, rich dipping chocolate, often enjoyed for breakfast or a late-night snack. In Catalunya, the signature dessert is Crema Catalana, a creamy custard topped with a layer of hard caramel, similar to the French crème brûlée.

Further south, in Andalusia, you'll find Piononos, small sweet pastries typical of the province of Granada. Named after Pope Pius IX, these delicious cakes are traditionally caramelized on the outside, creamy on the inside, and often served with a dusting of powdered sugar on top.

To truly appreciate the array of Spanish desserts, visit local bakeries or 'pastelerías' where these sweet delicacies are freshly made. You can also sample a variety of these treats in most traditional Spanish restaurants. Alternatively, for those interested in honing their culinary skills, consider taking a cooking class specializing in Spanish desserts. It's a fun, engaging way to learn about the country's sweet traditions.

Spain's Food Markets

Spain's food markets are more than just places to shop; they're vibrant, bustling hubs where locals and tourists alike can experience the rich tapestry of Spanish cuisine. From the world-renowned Mercado de la Boqueria in Barcelona to the Mercado Central in Valencia, these markets offer an abundance of fresh produce, local specialties, and culinary delights.

Stalls brim with colorful fruits and vegetables, freshly caught seafood, artisan cheeses, and an array of cured meats, including the prized Jamón Ibérico. Many markets also feature tapas bars and food stalls, where you can enjoy freshly prepared meals made from ingredients sourced directly from the market.

Visiting a local food market is a must when traveling in Spain. It's a chance to see where the locals shop, learn about regional produce, and perhaps sample some culinary treats. Remember to respect local customs, such as waiting your turn and taking small amounts if you're sampling. And don't forget to bring a shopping bag - you never know what delicious goodies you might want to take with you!

Vegetarian and Vegan Options

While Spain is often associated with meat and seafood dishes, the country's culinary landscape has expanded over the years to cater to vegetarian and vegan diets. Many traditional Spanish dishes are plant-based, like Gazpacho and Pisto, a sort of Spanish ratatouille. Tapas bars often offer vegetarian options such as Pimientos de Padrón (fried green peppers) or Patatas Bravas (spicy potatoes).

Increasingly, cities like Madrid, Barcelona, and Valencia are witnessing a rise in vegetarian and vegan eateries, ranging from casual cafés to gourmet restaurants. In addition, many regular restaurants now offer vegetarian and vegan alternatives on their menus.

When dining out, don't hesitate to ask the staff for vegetarian or vegan options—they are usually accommodating and can recommend suitable dishes. For those looking to prepare their own meals, health food stores and local markets offer a variety of plant-based ingredients. Ultimately, even as a vegetarian or vegan, you can enjoy the gastronomic richness that Spain has to offer.

Sustainable Food Practices

In recent years, Spain has been undergoing a transformation in its approach to food production and consumption. More and more, sustainability and eco-consciousness are becoming integral to the country's culinary landscape. This shift is most noticeable in the surge of organic farming, with Spain leading Europe in organic vineyards and olive groves.

Spain's traditional practices, such as seasonality and the emphasis on local ingredients, align perfectly with sustainable food practices. The trend of "zero kilometer" dining, which promotes using locally sourced ingredients to reduce food miles, is gaining popularity in restaurants across the country.

When traveling in Spain, look for restaurants and markets that highlight local, seasonal, and organic products. Opting for such establishments not only supports local communities but also allows you to taste food at its freshest and most flavorful. You'll also find a growing number of organic stores and farmers markets, which are worth visiting to appreciate the variety and quality of Spanish produce.

Final Thoughts

Reflecting on the cuisine of Spain, it's evident that the country is not just a destination for the palate but also a journey into centuries-old traditions, the richness of diverse cultures, and a growing consciousness towards sustainability. The culinary experience is so integral to the Spanish lifestyle that to truly understand the country, one must dive headfirst into its food and drink.

The city of Seville, not previously mentioned in this chapter, is renowned for its vibrant food scene. The Triana Market, located in the heart of Seville's traditional Triana neighborhood, offers an array of Andalusian specialities. Also, remember to try the city's famous orange wine, a sweet and aromatic accompaniment to any meal.

Spanish cuisine, however, extends beyond the boundaries of mainland Spain. The Canary Islands, for instance, offer a unique culinary identity with dishes like "papas arrugadas" (wrinkled potatoes) served with mojo sauce, while the Balearic Islands are known for "sobrasada", a type of cured sausage.

Remember to be adventurous with your food choices. Whether it's sampling "morcilla" (blood sausage) in Burgos, trying the anchovies in Cantabria, or savoring the delectable Basque pintxos, each region offers something distinct and memorable. A trip to Spain, for the food lover, is like an interactive, open-air museum where you can taste history, culture, and the vibrant soul of Spain. So venture forth, armed with a curious palate and an adventurous spirit, to savour Spain's diverse and rich culinary landscape. Spain is truly a food lover's paradise.

CHAPTER 11:
How to Travel Spain on a Budget

Spain, a country brimming with world-renowned landmarks, captivating cultures, and delicious cuisine, doesn't have to be an expensive destination. With a bit of planning and some savvy choices, you can enjoy the Spanish charm without exhausting your wallet. From budget-friendly accommodations to affordable dining options, Spain offers numerous ways to explore the country on a budget.

Being conscious about your travel expenses doesn't mean skimping on experiences. Many of Spain's attractions can be explored inexpensively or even for free. Moreover, travelling on a budget often brings you closer to local life, as you explore traditional markets, eat where locals eat, and use public transportation.

The following sections provide practical tips and suggestions to help you plan your Spanish adventure on a budget. From finding affordable accommodation to savouring cheap local eats, these strategies will ensure your journey through Spain is economical yet still rich with experiences.

Budget Accommodation

Spain offers a wide range of budget-friendly accommodation options, which can significantly reduce your travel expenses. Hostels are an excellent choice for budget travellers. Not only do they offer inexpensive dormitory-style rooms, but they also often include amenities like communal kitchens where you can prepare meals, helping you save further on food costs.

Another economical accommodation option in Spain are "pensiones" or guest houses, which provide basic facilities at a reasonable price. They are often family-run and offer a more intimate and local experience compared to larger hotels.

For those who prefer more privacy, consider booking an apartment or a room through online platforms like Airbnb. This is especially cost-effective for longer stays or if you're travelling in a group. Always check the reviews and the location before booking to ensure it meets your needs and expectations.

Eating on a Budget

One of the joys of travelling in Spain is the country's delectable cuisine. Thankfully, enjoying Spanish food doesn't have to be expensive. Tapas bars are a perfect example of how you can eat well on a budget. In many places, especially in the southern region of Andalusia, a free tapa is still served with each drink you order.

Spain's food markets are another excellent option for cheap eats. Here you can sample a variety of local products without spending a lot. Some markets, like Madrid's Mercado de San Miguel or Barcelona's La Boqueria, even have bars and stalls serving prepared meals at a reasonable price.

Another tip to eat cheaply in Spain is to take advantage of the "menu del dia" or menu of the day. This is a set lunch, usually including a starter, main course, dessert, and a drink, often for under 15 euros. It's widely available in restaurants across the country, particularly on weekdays.

Public Transport

Spain's public transportation system is efficient, reliable, and can be a cost-effective way to navigate the country. In cities like Madrid, Barcelona, Valencia, and Seville, buses, trams, and metros form a comprehensive network that can take you just about anywhere you need to go. Many cities offer transport cards that provide unlimited travel for a specific time period, typically 24 hours, 48 hours, or a week, which can save money if you plan to use public transport frequently.

For intercity travel, Spain's long-distance bus network is extensive and often cheaper than trains or flights. Companies like ALSA operate routes across the country. If you prefer trains, consider booking in advance or travelling at less popular times to secure the best fares. Spain's high-speed AVE trains are more expensive, but regional trains offer a budget-friendly alternative. Cycling is another affordable way to get around, particularly in bike-friendly cities like Barcelona or Seville. Many cities have bike-sharing schemes, and rentals are typically reasonably priced. Just remember to wear a helmet and follow local traffic rules.

Free Attractions

Exploring Spain's rich cultural heritage doesn't have to cost a fortune. Many cities offer free or discounted entry to museums and monuments at certain times. For example, the Prado Museum in Madrid and the Picasso Museum in Barcelona both offer free entry during certain hours. It's worth checking the official websites of attractions for up-to-date information on admission fees and "free entry" hours.

Walking tours are a great way to see the city highlights without spending a lot. There are free walking tours available in many Spanish cities - these are typically tip-based, so you can pay what you feel the tour was worth.

Moreover, don't overlook the many free experiences Spain has to offer: strolling through the historic Barrio Gótico in Barcelona, exploring the vibrant street art in Madrid's Malasaña district, or watching a sunset from the beach in Costa del Sol. Sometimes, the best things in life really are free.

Budget Shopping

Spain offers various options for those looking to shop on a budget. Street markets are a great place to start. From clothing and accessories to vintage goods and antiques, you can find a wide variety of items at a bargain price. El Rastro in Madrid and Els Encants in Barcelona are among the country's most famous markets.

For affordable fashion, look no further than Spanish high-street brands like Zara, Mango, and Bershka. They often have sales, particularly during the summer and after Christmas, when you can score high-quality clothes and accessories at a discount.

Also, keep in mind that many cities in Spain have "Mercadillos" or weekly street markets where locals shop for fresh produce, clothes, and household items at lower prices. It's a fantastic way to blend in with the locals while hunting for deals. Lastly, remember that bargaining is generally acceptable at markets, so don't be afraid to negotiate the price!

Cheap Flight and Train Tips

In Spain, flying or taking a train can be a cost-effective mode of transport, particularly if you're traveling long distances or across the country. For flights, budget airlines such as Ryanair and Vueling offer competitive prices, especially if you can be flexible with your travel dates and book in advance. Keep an eye out for promotions and deals, and consider signing up for airlines' newsletters for exclusive offers.

For train travel, Renfe, the Spanish national train company, provides high-speed AVE trains connecting major cities like Madrid, Barcelona, and Seville. To get the best prices, try to book your tickets as soon as they're released (usually 60 days before departure), especially for popular routes. Also, consider traveling on less busy days or times, such as midweek or early in the morning, to get cheaper fares.

Discount Cards

Various cities in Spain offer discount cards, which can help you save money on attractions, public transport, and even dining. For example, the Barcelona Card offers free public transport and free or discounted entry to many of the city's top attractions. Similarly, Madrid's Tourist Card provides unlimited public transport and discounts on sightseeing tours, shows, and shopping.

Besides city cards, Spain also offers the Spain Pass for train travel, which allows a certain number of journeys within a set period, providing excellent value if you plan to travel extensively by train. Remember to compare the cost of the card with your planned activities to ensure it's worth the investment.

Off-Season Travel

Timing your trip wisely can save you a significant amount of money. Spain's peak tourist season is summer, particularly in coastal areas and popular cities. By traveling off-season (generally from October to April, excluding Christmas and Easter), you'll find lower prices on accommodation and flights, fewer crowds, and a more relaxed atmosphere.

Weather-wise, Spanish winters are relatively mild, and you can still enjoy plenty of sunshine in the south. For skiing enthusiasts, winter is the perfect time to hit the slopes in the Sierra Nevada or the Pyrenees, while autumn and spring are ideal for city trips or hiking adventures.

Final Thoughts

Traveling Spain on a budget does not mean missing out on the wonders this country has to offer. In fact, with careful planning and savvy choices, the vibrant cities, rich history, and diverse landscapes of Spain become an affordable reality. Don't forget to take advantage of Spain's delightful and affordable gastronomy, from tapas bars to local markets, where you can sample regional specialties without breaking the bank.

Remember that some of the best experiences are often free or low-cost - a walk through the historic quarters, a picnic in a beautiful park, a stunning sunset by the beach. So, embrace the adventure, for Spain is a country where priceless memories can be made, regardless of budget. With these tips in hand, the dream of a Spanish escape is well within your reach. Safe travels and enjoy every moment of your journey!

CHAPTER 12:
10 Cultural Experiences You Must Try in Spain

Embracing Spanish culture goes far beyond just visiting the sights; it's about experiencing the vibrancy and passion of Spain's traditions, arts, sports, and language. From the energetic flamenco performances and the national fervor of a football match to the nuanced flavours of Spanish wines and the country's rich artistic heritage, the Spanish culture is a lively tapestry of diverse and fascinating experiences.

Immerse yourself in the joy of Spanish festivals, filled with color, music, and a strong sense of community. Witness the controversy and tradition of bullfighting, an integral part of Spain's cultural fabric, despite the debates surrounding it. Explore the legacy of Spanish artists, whose masterpieces have left a lasting imprint on the world's art scene.

Take the opportunity to taste Spain's renowned wines in their native setting, learn about the nation's traditional crafts, and even attempt speaking Spanish. Each of these experiences offers a unique insight into the Spanish way of life, deepening your connection with the country and its people. So, let's embark on this exciting journey and explore some unforgettable cultural experiences in Spain!

1 - Flamenco Show

The pulsating rhythm of a flamenco show is an experience that captures the essence of Spain's passionate spirit. The rapid-fire footwork of the dancers, the soulful strumming of the guitar, and the powerful voice of the singer combine to create an atmosphere that's both electrifying and deeply emotional. Flamenco is not just a dance or a genre of music; it's an expressive art form that embodies the resilience, fervour, and vibrancy of the Spanish people.

Flamenco shows can be found all across Spain, but Andalusia, particularly the cities of Seville, Granada, and Jerez, is the birthplace and the heartland of flamenco. The tablaos (flamenco venues) here offer an intimate setting where the raw intensity of flamenco can be felt up close. Remember to book in advance as these shows are quite popular.

2 - Spanish Fiestas

Spanish fiestas are the epitome of Spain's exuberant culture, a splendid display of tradition, community spirit, and celebration. From the famous Running of the Bulls in Pamplona to the messy revelry of La Tomatina in Buñol and the fiery Las Fallas in Valencia, each fiesta has its unique character and allure, though all are equally vibrant and full of life.

The best way to enjoy a Spanish fiesta is to join in. Immerse yourself in the festivities, whether that means running ahead of a herd of bulls, tossing tomatoes at fellow revelers, or admiring the intricate ninots (statues) at Las Fallas. Each city and region has its own calendar of festivals, so be sure to check the local schedules when planning your visit.

3 - Bullfighting

Bullfighting, or la corrida, is one of the most traditional and controversial aspects of Spanish culture. To some, it's a captivating spectacle and an art form deeply rooted in Spanish history; to others, it's a contentious sport that raises ethical issues. Regardless of one's perspective, there's no denying the impact of bullfighting on Spanish culture.

Bullfighting season in Spain runs from March to October, with events taking place in bullrings across the country. The most famous bullring is Madrid's Las Ventas, a stunning Moorish-style arena. If you choose to attend a bullfight, be prepared for a display of dramatic theatre, skilled athleticism, and powerful emotions. However, be aware of the intense and, at times, graphic nature of the event.

4 - Spanish Art

Spain's art scene is as diverse and colourful as the country itself, boasting a rich history that has given rise to some of the world's most renowned artists. From the masterpieces of the Golden Age painters like Velázquez and El Greco to the modernist works of Picasso, Dalí, and Miró, Spanish art offers an eclectic array of styles and periods to explore.

Madrid's Golden Triangle of Art, consisting of the Prado Museum, the Reina Sofia Museum, and the Thyssen-Bornemisza Museum, is a must-visit for any art lover. However, Spanish art is not just confined to museums and galleries. The incredible architecture of Gaudí in Barcelona, the hauntingly beautiful cave paintings in Altamira, and the colourful murals in Valencia's street art district reflect the country's artistic spirit in every corner.

5 - Wine Tasting

Spain is a country of diverse landscapes, climates, and soils, a combination that makes it one of the world's top wine-producing countries. From the robust reds of Rioja and Ribera del Duero to the crisp whites of Rías Baixas and the sparkling cava of Penedès, Spanish wines are as varied as they are delicious.

The best way to appreciate Spanish wines is by visiting the country's numerous wine regions, where you can tour centuries-old vineyards, learn about the wine-making process, and, of course, sample the wines. Many bodegas (wineries) offer guided tours and tastings, often paired with local cheeses, hams, and other regional delicacies. Remember to book in advance, especially during the harvest season from September to October.

6 - Traditional Crafts

Craftsmanship in Spain is a testament to the country's rich cultural heritage. From pottery and ceramics to leather goods and lace, traditional crafts reveal the artistic skills passed down through generations. Whether it's the colourful ceramics of Talavera and Seville, the intricate lacework of Tenerife, or the elegant damascene work of Toledo, each region has its own distinctive craft traditions.

Visiting local workshops and artisan markets is an excellent way to discover and support these age-old crafts. It's not only an opportunity to buy unique souvenirs but also a chance to meet the artisans, learn about their craft, and understand the history and cultural significance of their work. Make sure to explore the local craft scene when visiting cities like Granada, Valencia, and Seville.

7 - Spanish Language

Speaking Spanish, or at least making an attempt to, can significantly enrich your travel experience in Spain. As the second most widely spoken language in the world, Spanish opens the door to a wealth of cultural experiences and interactions. Not only does it enable you to engage more deeply with the locals, but it also offers insights into the Spanish way of life.

There are many ways to immerse yourself in the language during your trip. Consider enrolling in a short language course or attend language exchange events in cities like Madrid and Barcelona. Don't hesitate to practice your Spanish at every opportunity, be it at a local mercado (market), a flamenco show, or during a friendly encounter at a tapas bar.

8 - Spanish Sports

Spain is a country where sports are deeply embedded in the culture. From the passion of a football match to the adrenaline of a bullfight, the Spanish love for sports is contagious and engaging. Football is undeniably the most popular sport, with top clubs like Real Madrid and Barcelona attracting millions of fans from around the world.

Attending a football match at one of Spain's famous stadiums, such as Camp Nou or Santiago Bernabeu, is an unforgettable experience, filled with energy and passion. If football isn't your thing, there are plenty of other sports events to check out, including the San Fermín running of the bulls in Pamplona or the Conde de Godó Tennis Tournament in Barcelona.

9 - Spanish Music

Spanish music is as varied and diverse as the country itself. From the passionate flamenco rhythms of Andalusia and the haunting tunes of Galician bagpipes to the lively indie scene of Madrid and Barcelona, Spanish music is a true reflection of the country's regional diversity and rich cultural history.

Experiencing live music in Spain is not to be missed. Attend a flamenco show in Seville, explore the vibrant nightlife and music scene of Madrid and Barcelona, or enjoy traditional Basque music in San Sebastián. There's also a host of music festivals throughout the year, catering to a wide range of musical tastes.

10 - Spanish Architecture

Spain's architecture is a captivating blend of diverse styles, reflecting the many cultures that have shaped the country's history. From the grandeur of Madrid's Royal Palace and Barcelona's stunning modernist buildings by Gaudí to the intricate Islamic designs of Granada's Alhambra and the avant-garde architecture of Bilbao's Guggenheim Museum, each city offers a unique architectural experience.

Taking a guided architectural tour can deepen your understanding of the historical and cultural contexts behind these architectural wonders. Also, don't miss the chance to explore Spain's less-touristy regions, such as Extremadura and Navarre, where you can discover Roman ruins, medieval fortresses, and charming rural architecture.

Conclusion

As we arrive at the conclusion of this guide, it's almost overwhelming to look back and reflect upon the vibrant tapestry that is Spain. Each region, each city, each tiny pueblo has its own unique allure, drawing us in with its distinct character and charm. But more than the sum of its individual parts, it's the overarching spirit of Spain - that irresistible zest for life - that truly captivates. Spain is more than a destination; it's a way of life, a sensory delight, an enchanting story written in the language of sunlit days and starry nights, reverberating Flamenco rhythms, and the warm, hearty laughter of its people.

Spain's allure is indeed intoxicating, but remember that the essence of travel isn't merely about checking off a list of sights or activities. It's about immersing yourself in the local culture, engaging with the people, and opening your senses to new experiences and perspectives. And Spain offers a myriad of opportunities for such meaningful engagements, whether it's sipping on a glass of smooth Rioja in a bustling tapas bar, soaking in the sacred aura of a centuries-old cathedral, or finding yourself lost in a cobblestoned alley adorned with vibrant ceramic tiles and hanging geraniums.

Remember that in Spain, it's not just about where you go; it's also about when you go. Time your visit to coincide with a local fiesta or a cultural event for an authentic experience that will leave a lasting impression. There's something happening all year round, from the raucous Tomatina in August and the passionate Semana Santa processions in April to the stunning fallas of Valencia in March and the vibrant Feria de Abril in Seville. These events offer an unparalleled opportunity to dive into Spanish traditions and customs, far beyond the usual tourist track.

Exploring Spain doesn't have to be an expensive affair. Embrace the local way of life to save money and enrich your experience. This could mean opting for a 'menú del día' at lunch, taking advantage of the free entrance times at many museums, shopping at local markets, or using public transport to get around. Don't hesitate to step off the beaten path - some of the most rewarding experiences often lie away from the main tourist routes.

As for the language, don't worry if you don't speak fluent Spanish. While learning a few basic phrases can go a long way in creating a connection with the locals, Spaniards are generally friendly and patient, even when faced with a language barrier. And who knows? You might find yourself picking up more Spanish than you expected by the end of your trip.

To help you along the way, here are some basic phrases that can be useful for any traveller in Spain:

▷ ¿Dónde está...? (Where is...?)

▷ ¿Cuánto cuesta? (How much does it cost?)

▷ ¿Habla inglés? (Do you speak English?)

▷ ¿Puede ayudarme? (Can you help me?)

▷ No entiendo. (I don't understand.)

▷ Estoy perdido/a. (I'm lost.)

- ¿Dónde está el baño? (Where is the bathroom?)

- ¿Podría ver el menú, por favor? (Could I see the menu, please?)

- Me gustaría... (I would like...)

- Gracias. (Thank you.)

- De nada. (You're welcome.)

- Por favor. (Please.)

- Disculpe. (Excuse me.)

- ¿Cómo se llama esto? (What is this called?)

- ¿Cómo llego a...? (How do I get to...?)

Remember, it's the effort and the intention to communicate that often matters more than perfect grammar or pronunciation. So don't be afraid to try out your Spanish - it's all part of the adventure!

Spain's culinary scene is a joy to discover, as much for the gourmet as for the casual food lover. Tapas hopping is a delicious and sociable affair, paella is a celebration in a pan, and the seafood, particularly in coastal regions, is simply out of this world. Remember that meal times in Spain are usually later than in many other countries, so adapt to the local rhythm to truly savour the gastronomic delights that Spain has to offer.

In Spain, art and culture aren't confined to museums or galleries; they're everywhere, in the flamboyant architecture, the age-old traditions, the passionate music and dance, and even in the way the Spanish enjoy their free time. Spain's cultural wealth is indeed astounding, and no matter how much time you spend here, there will always be something new to discover, to marvel at, to fall in love with.

Lastly, travel slow and savour every moment. Spain is not a place to be rushed. It's a place to linger over a leisurely lunch, to siesta in the shade of an olive tree, to stroll along a golden beach as the sun sets, to dance the night away under a sky full of stars. It's a place to live the moment, to feel the pulse of life, to breathe in the air of history and tradition, and to let the Spanish spirit seep into your soul.

With its rich cultural tapestry, mesmerizing landscapes, soul-stirring art and music, vibrant cities, and gastronomic delights, Spain promises an unforgettable travel experience. But remember, Spain isn't just a place to visit; it's a place to experience, to savour, and to love. So, pack your bags, bring an open heart, and embark on the Spanish adventure that awaits you. And as you set foot on Spanish soil, remember the words of the famous Spanish proverb: "Con paciencia y saliva, el elefante se la metió a la hormiga" - with patience and perseverance, you can achieve anything.

Here's to a journey of a lifetime in Spain, a journey that will linger in your heart and soul long after you've returned home.

Final notes

You have reached the end of your journey through Spain, probably one of the most appreciated destinations among travelers from all over the world. We hope that the suggested destinations and our advice will help you plan and enjoy your trip to the fullest.

The travel guide series of the Journey Joy collection was designed to be lean and straight to the point. The idea of keeping the guides short required significant work in synthesis, in order to guide the reader towards the essential destinations and activities within each country and city.

If you liked the book, leaving a positive review can help us spread our work. We realize that leaving a review can be a tedious activity, so we want to give you a gift. Send an email to **bonus@dedaloagency.net**, attach the screenshot of your review, and you will get completely **FREE**, in your mailbox, **THE UNRELEASED EBOOK**: "The Art of Traveling: Essential Tips for Unforgettable Journeys".

Remember to check the Spam folder, as the email might end up there!

We thank you in advance and wish you to always travel and enjoy every adventure!

Made in the USA
Coppell, TX
17 November 2024

40401758R00111